THE GREAT BOOK
OF BASEBALL

Interesting Facts
and Sports Stories

Sports Trivia Vol.3

Bill O'Neill
&
Ryan Black

ISBN: 978-1-64845-019-8

DON'T FORGET YOUR
FREE BOOKS

CONTENTS

INTRODUCTION

Whether you're a young man that thinks the Chicago Cubs win the World Series all the time, or someone more seasoned that remembers routinely scheduled double-headers, there's plenty of food at the table in this book. It's is an eclectic collection that's part Ripley's' Believe It or Not, and part Guinness Book of World Records, combined with some candid humor and fun trivia. For some it's an educational experience, and for others it'll bring back memories. Some of those memories will be good or bad, depending on who you were rooting for at the time!

If you want to go past the headlines or beyond the common perceptions, and have some fun doing it, then this baseball book was written for you!

Doubleday is credited with having invented baseball back in 1839, although some dispute that. However, baseball's Hall of Fame is built in Cooperstown, NY, where supposedly the first game was played. Much of the game is played the same way today, or 178 years later. And of course there are some components of the game that have long since been archived. Baseball went from a little boys games to the "national pastime". It went from something that was a mere hobby to something that is watched live by millions. Ask yourself where baseball would be today without inventions such as the radio, television, and of course the internet.

Technology and money have changed the game perhaps more than any other external force, and let me share a true story to with you. Ten years ago the Miami Marlins were playing the Mets in New York. It was a chilly day in late September. Miami had long since been eliminated from playoff contention. As the players were on the bus from the hotel to the park, many of them took to their Twitter accounts to express how cold it was, how they'd rather be anywhere but stuck in New York traffic, and some were making golf reservations in Miami upon their return home.

It was evident they didn't want to play a baseball game! I said to a friend that if I were a gambling man I'd bet the mortgage on the Mets, who promptly won the game 13-0. Now, that kind of "talk" has gone on for years, but with Twitter it became instant information.

We're closer to our favorite players than ever, we know more about their personal lives than we care to know, and often times we can see things on television as it happens that players cannot!

It wasn't always like that, so we'll look at some people who made the game, some people who changed the game, and some classic moments that some of you will know exactly where you were when they happened. It's a deep-dive into baseball history, trivia, and interesting/fun facts for everyone. Some of the guys did enough to make the book more than once. We hope you enjoy reading as much as we did writing!

CHAPTER ONE:

LEGENDS

People living in the most remote areas of the world will leave a mark on the world in some way. That would include everyone! But baseball players tend to leave bigger marks because they're in a bigger spotlight. Often times the legacy they leave is an unintended consequence and not their biggest achievement. There are literally scores of people that could have made Chapter One a novel in and of itself, so we chose the more recognizable names that span several generations.

Ted Williams

Aside from being one of the most prolific hitters of all time, in 1942, in what was to be the prime of his career, he was drafted into the military and spent four years on active duty.

Upon his discharge in 1946 he rejoined the Boston Red Sox, signing a contract for $37,500, which in today's dollars would equate to $496,000! We can call that "mere" because in the year 2107 the minimum Major League Baseball salary is $535,000.

What's more astonishing about The Splendid Splinter (his nickname) is that upon his death his son and youngest daughter chose to have his remains frozen cryogenically. They were, and they were sent to Alcor, a Scottsdale-based Life Extension company that as of this writing has 149 people in "cryopreservation."

Pete Rose

Named "Charlie Hustle" for his tenacious play on the field, Pete Rose is baseball's all-time hit leader with 4256 of them. Pete played 25 years in MLB, most of them with the Cincinnati Reds, and managed the Reds from 1984-1989.

Rose played in the All-Star game seventeen times, was a three-time batting champion, and was a World Series Most Valuable Player, his team having won the Series three times.

In spite of those lofty accomplishments, Pete was banned from baseball for gambling, as much as $10,000 per day, and on or against his own team. And in 1990 he pled guilty to filing false tax returns, some of which was failure to report winnings from betting on horse races.

Shoeless Joe Jackson

Joe got the nickname "Shoeless" during a mill game he played in Greenville, SC. He took off a new pair of cleats that were giving him blisters, then proceeded to run the bases in his socks. To this day he maintains the third highest career batting average of anyone in baseball history, and in 1999 a Sporting News poll voted him 35th on a list of the Top 100 players of ALL TIME, and he still holds franchise records in Cleveland and Chicago!

And yet, he is not in Cooperstown, the home of the Hall of Fame.

Sadly, he is most remembered for his alleged role in the Black Sox scandal, when he and his teammates allegedly "threw" the World Series to the Cincinnati Reds in 1919. As a result of the alleged conspiracy, the first Commissioner of MLB, Kennesaw Landis, banned him from the game for life, and being on the ineligible list precludes his election to the Hall of Fame.

Deion Sanders

Most younger people know him as a broadcast analyst for CBS Sports and the National Football League, and he is often referred to as "Prime Time". However, from 1989 to 1997 he played on and off for five different Major League Baseball teams! In fact, he later made a comeback of sorts, playing 29 games with the Cincinnati Reds in 2001!

Deion played in the 1992 World Series for the Atlanta Braves, batted .533 with 8 hits, despite playing with a broken bone in his foot. He couldn't have had that foot injury all year, since he led the Reds in triples that season.

During his career he had 186 stolen bases, has since been elected to the Pro Football Hall of Fame, and is still the only player to have played in a Super Bowl and in a World Series.

Cal Ripken, Jr.

In 1995 Cal Ripken broke a record held previously held by Lou Gehrig for most consecutive games played (2130) and ended his streak voluntarily in 1998 at 2632 straight games. He was given the nickname "The Iron Man", which is somewhat self-explanatory, but it is also a spinoff of Gehrig's also-known-as, "The Iron Horse".

Some say that may be a record that will never be broken, and given that the average baseball career is slightly less than six years (roughly 972 games) it is quite possibly true.

His record-breaking game on September 6th of that year and still stands as one of ESPN's most watched baseball games. Both President Bill Clinton and Vice President Al Gore were in attendance, and in fact, President Clinton was in the broadcast booth in the 4th inning and called had the honor of calling a Cal Ripken home run.

Jackie Robinson

There is a first for everything and everything has a first. Jackie Robinson was the first African American Major League Baseball player, and this didn't happen until 1947. That does seem like a long time ago. To be precise it was 70 years ago, and a full 27 years before Boston had forced busing desegregation. That is just putting it into some sort of perspective for you.

To put that in better context, slavery was abolished in 1865, so it wasn't until 82 years LATER we had an African American in Major

League Baseball, which was invented in 1839, according to many.

Jackie wasn't brought up by the Brooklyn Dodgers as a token African American, either. He was Rookie if the Year in 1947 and a six-time All-Star.

Jim "Catfish"Hunter

Jim Hunter was perhaps best known during his career for the big handlebar moustache he sported and probably because he spent a number of years with the New York Yankees. Anyone who plays any sport in New York becomes bigger than life simply because of the massive amount of media coverage.

But the real story with Catfish Hunter was how he ended up Yankees. He had been with the A's and their outspoken owner Charlie Finley, who had always been quite frugal. After refusing to re-up his contract, Catfish won an arbitration hearing to become what was in effect the first real "free agent".

Sadly he developed ALS and passed away in 1999 at the age of 53. His legacy was so important to so many that Bob Dylan wrote a song in his honor, simply titled, "Catfish". Jim has also been the subject of or referred to in many famous movies, perhaps most notably "The Bad News Bears", with Walter Matthau and Tatum O'Neal.

Bob Gibson

1968 was called "The Year of the Pitcher" and in no small part to the season Gibson had. He posted a 1.12 ERA which was by a landslide the lowest in 54 years. He won the Cy Young Award as the National League Most Valuable Pitcher, and also won the award as the most valuable player. That wouldn't happen again until Clayton Kershaw did it in 2014.

That feat was directly responsible for the league lowering the mound AND tightening up the strike zone. Prior to 1968 the mound had been 15" (and many teams were accused of keeping it even higher) and it was subsequently lowered a full 5". It hasn't changed since.

In 2004 Fox Sports named him the most intimidating pitcher of all time!

George Brett

Brett was one of the best third-baseman to play the game, and for full twenty years. During that time he won numerous batting titles and was an All-Star 13 times. He took the Kansas City Royals to the World Series and won in 1985, but he may be best remembered for "The Pine Tar Incident".

Brett had just hit a home run off of another Hall of Famer, Goose Gossage, to put the Royals ahead in the ninth inning. Yankee manager Billy Martin (another character for another chapter!) challenged the rule that said "no foreign substance should extend more than 18" from the knob of the bat." Although pine tar was perfectly legal, the umpire measured the bat and found the tar to be 24" beyond the knob, called Brett out, and ended the game.

Kansas City promptly protested, and it was subsequently upheld, so the game was later resumed from the point of the home run. I could only imagine Billy Martin sitting in the dugout waiting for just the right time to pull that rule out. He had to know!

Barry Bonds

When I was young I collected baseball cards like most young boys did. Sometimes I shudder to think of the value of the ones I ruined between my bicycle spokes, but Barry's rookie card wasn't one of them. In fact, I still have it. When he broke Hank Aaron's home run record I thought I was sitting on a goldmine!

I look at that card today and see this skinny young guy in a Pirates uniform, the son of another baseball great, Bobby Bonds. Bobby used to kill my Red Sox. Then I look at the Barry Bonds on television that played for the San Francisco Giants and wonder what the heck happened. That dude is Mr. T on steroids. Well, I wasn't far off.

Although it was never formally proven that he used steroids knowingly, he was indicted on perjury charges that he lied under oath about his use of them, which was all part of what' is known as the Balco scandal. It's assumed that where there is smoke there is fire, and two years later all four defendants in the Balco trial struck deals with the prosecution that didn't require them to name names, for simplification purposes.

As of now, and even with the all-time home run record, he is not in the Hall of Fame and it is clearly because of HOF voter bias, and who can blame them. Bonds is not alone in that category of players who had great contributions to the game and deserving of HOF consideration that remain on the outside looking in.

Alex Rodriguez

Alex was very closely tied to the whole steroid issue as well. He has been interviewed on 60 Minutes (among others) and after years of denial admitted to using steroids. He said it was for only three years due to the pressure to perform, but most think that it is likely much longer than that.

However, that is not what Alex did to change the game. It is that pressure to perform thing. Alex had one of the most aggressive agents in baseball, Scott Boras. In fact, Boras is still quite active. He and Alex held up the Texas Rangers for a 10-year contract worth over a quarter of a billion dollars, or $170,000 per game. To put that in perspective the next most lucrative contract at the time was a full $63 million less. That changed everything going forward, as it forced the league to expand the revenue sharing contract it had in place to assure small market teams the ability to compete.

Its effects are still being felt. Giancarlo Stanton of the Marlins recently signed a 13 year, $325 million contract, and he hasn't done nearly enough to justify that by most standards. But Miami was simply forced to pay him the money or lose the face of the franchise, what few fans they have in South Florida, and basically their relevance as a business. It is the same business that is about to sell for $1.6 billion bucks!

Babe Ruth's 1918 contract was for $5000. The actual contract itself sold in 2014 for a little over a million dollars!

Ichiro Suzuki

Known simply as "Ichiro," Suzuki played from 1992 through 2000 for the Orix Blue Wave in the Nippon Professional Baseball League in Japan. He was such a dominant player that teams in the US were salivating at the chance to sign him. A year prior to him being eligible for free agency in Japan, the Orix had become a cash-poor cellar-dweller and sold the rights to negotiate with him to the Seattle Mariners for $13 million. The rights, not the contract. Eventually the Mariners did indeed sign him to play in the US, and his contract to play baseball was for three years at $14 million, or a lot less than just the rights to talk to him!

Over the years (and he's still playing for Miami) he was well worth what Seattle had to cough up. So much so that nearly every other team in Major League Baseball set up an entire arm of their scouting organization dedicated to Japan entirely, all in an effort to find "the next Suzuki".

Since that initial dam broke with Ichiro coming over, there have been many successful players from Japan, and nearly all of them have been very expensive bets by the franchises. Bets that teams only HOPE these new Japanese players can duplicate their success across the Pacific back here in Major League Baseball.

Ty Cobb

Not many (perhaps none) people reading this saw Ty Cobb play, but my guess is that most true baseball fans have heard of him. He spent the majority of his career as both a player and a manager for the Detroit Tigers, ending his tenure in 1926.

He was a tremendous player, winning the League Most Valuable Player Award, the home run title, and was a twelve-time batting champion. Of course, that's what people will remember him best for, and well they should. And collectors sure do too, as one of his very rare baseball cards recently sold for over $1 million! And believe it or not it was actually found in an old grocery bag.

One thing about Ty Cobb most will concede, however, is that he had a wicked temper. In fact, in 1912 he assaulted a heckling (and apparently disabled) fan and was subsequently suspended for a period of time. His teammates also protested. The handling of that incident was a precursor to what we now know as the MLB Players Union, one of the most powerful unions in sports today.

Gaylord Perry

Perry pitched in Major League Baseball for over two decades, his career ending in 1983. He is one of only 24 pitchers to ever win 300 games, and with the specialization of pitching in the game today it is quite likely there won't ever be a 25th person on that list.

But what Gaylord Perry is perhaps most remembered for is throwing a "spitball." A spitball is nothing more than a pitch altered by a foreign substance, which causes the ball to move in an unpredictable manner, hence it's quite effective! The only problem with that is rule 8.02 states that "a pitcher may not apply a foreign substance to the ball." Spit balls were banned as far back as 1920, and yet even in recently there have been cases of pitchers were caught and immediately ejected from the game.

Perry admitted to using K-Y Jelly, Vaseline, saliva, and even sweat. It became such a cloud of him that even as umpires were trying to catch him and players were trying to hit him, the aura of what he MIGHT be doing became more of an edge that his actual abilities with the ball!

So, as Shakespeare once said, "the good that men do oft lies in their bones, the bad lives on forever." And cheating will be what is the legacy of Gaylord Perry, perhaps overshadowing his career accomplishments on the field.

Ralph Branca

Ralph played a dozen years of Major League baseball, beginning his career in 1944 with the Brooklyn Dodgers. The majority of those years were mostly unremarkable from a statistics point of view. He pitched in 322 games and gave up 149 home runs.

But, there is one of those long balls that will live in infamy. In 1951 the Giants ended the regular season tied with their cross-town rivals, the Giants. They were to play a best two-of-three series to decide the National League pennant.

The drama was intense. The two teams each won a game and then they played one for all the marbles. It was the bottom of the ninth inning, Branca's Dodgers with the lead, and Ralph comes in from the bullpen to face a relative unknown, Bobby Thompson, with two runners on base. Thompson promptly deposited one in the stands, giving the Giants the pennant. That home run is referred to as "The Shot Heard 'Round the World," and what the long-time Brooklyn Dodger legend will always be remembered for.

And there's more! Branca later learned that the Giants had stolen the signals for the two pitches he threw, and that was actually confirmed by the Wall Street Journal in a 2001 article.

There is an upside, though. The moment that linked Bobby Thompson and Ralph Branca together forever is so well-known that for years the two have attended trade shows and signed memorabilia together, quite likely profiting far more than they did playing baseball.

RANDOM FUN FACTS

1. In 1919 eight members of the Chicago White Sox were accused of taking money from gamblers/gangsters to intentionally lose the World Series. The Black Sox scandal, as it came to be known, it still perhaps the biggest "fixing" controversy in sports.

2. It is possible for a pitcher to be credited with a win in a game and never throw a pitch. He can come on in the top of the 9th inning with his team tied or behind, pick a runner off of a base, and his team goes on to win in the game in the bottom of the 9th!

3. Jim "Catfish" Hunter was given the nickname by the Oakland A's owner, Charlie Finley, thinking he needed a catchy title. He was the first pitcher since 1915 to win 200 games by the age of 31.

4. In 1935 the Cincinnati Reds beat the Philadelphia Phillies 2-1 in the first night game. In wasn't until August of 1988 that Wrigley Field, the home of the Chicago Cubs since 1914, played under the lights.

5. In 1965, Bert Campaneris of the Oakland Athletics became the first player in history to play all nine positions in one game. Since then, it has been done three more times.

6. In 1973 the Oakland A's played a game with orange baseballs. It was an exhibition game and that is where the orange ended, as hitters complained they couldn't see the seams, hence the rotation of the ball.

7. Today, everyone has a mascot dancing on the dugout! The first one was introduced by the New York Mets in 1964, an odd looking thing they unveiled when they opened Shea Stadium.

8. Free entrance to baseball games for women, known of course as Ladies Day, was introduced in 1883 and was part of marketing for some teams until the mid-1950's. The average ticket price in the 1920's was about $1, and today the average price for spending a day at the park for two is about $78!

9. Between 1876 and 1888, Bill Holbert set a record that still stands today. He had 2335 at bats and did not hit a home run. Of course, the balls weren't juiced.

10. Rickey Henderson is the career leader in stolen bases with 1406. Ricky Henderson was also CAUGHT stealing 335 times, which is the record for most failed attempts.

11. As we said, Pete Rose is the all-time hit leader In baseball. Along the same theory as the Ricky Henderson stolen base record, Pete has also made the most OUTS in baseball history. The man with the second most outs is Hank Aaron.

12. Eddie Gaedel of the White Sox strolled up as a pinch-hitter in a game back in 1951. Pinch hitters are common, but not ones

that stand 3'7" tall! It was an intentional ploy by Chicago owner Bill Veeck to draw a walk, and it worked. Gaedel is officially listed as the shortest player ever to play in MLB.

13. The term "warning track" actually came about by accident. In the old Yankee Stadium there was a running track built for track and field events. Very soon outfielders realized it was a great "warning" for when they were about to crash into the wall!

14. The Baltimore Orioles are one of the most well knows teams, but what most probably don't know is that they were the original Milwaukee Brewers for one year before moving to St. Louis (and called the Browns) in 1902.

15. Bo Jackson won the College Football Heisman Trophy as the best player in the nation and was THE first pick in the 1986 NFL Draft. But from 1986-1994 he played for three MLB teams and made the All-Star team in 1989 playing for the Royals. Bo knows.

16. Jim Abbott was born without a right hand. He also had a ten-year career pitching (clearly left-handed) for a handful of teams, and tossed a no-hitter in 1993 while with the Yankees.

17. The fastest pitch ever recorded was thrown by Aroldis Chapman in 2010, and clocked at 105.1 MPH.

18. The most expensive baseball card ever is a 1909 T206 Series Honus Wagner. It sold for over five times the MLB minimum salary in 2107, or $2.8 million dollars.

19. The Miami Marlins are about to be sold. The reported selling price will be in the area of $1.6 billion dollars. That seems hefty for a team that hasn't been in the playoffs since 2003 and has one of the lowest attendances in MLB.

20. In 2012 ESPN and MLB agreed to a record-setting eight-year deal to keep baseball on the network until 2021. The agreement is worth $5.6 billion dollars.

TEST YOURSELF – QUESTIONS AND ANSWERS

1. In 1954 the Orioles moved from what city to Baltimore?

    A. Seattle
    B. St. Louis
    C. Washington

2. What player is nicknamed "The Iron Man" and played in 2632 consecutive games?

    A. Lou Gehrig
    B. Jackie Robinson
    C. Cal Ripken, Jr.

3. The Baseball Hall of Fame is in what city?

    A. Cooperstown, NY
    B. Canton, OH
    C. Baltimore, MD

4. Who is the only MLB player to appear in a World Series and play in a Super Bowl?

    A. Bo Jackson
    B. Deion Sanders
    C. Eddie Gaedel

5. Who was the first MLB team to introduce a mascot?

    A. New York Yankee
    B. Chicago Cubs
    C. New York Mets

ANSWERS

1. B
2. C
3. A
4. B
5. C

CHAPTER TWO:
THE ALL-STAR GAME

The Midsummer Classic, as it is often referred to, is the annual baseball celebrations game that for decades was simply a showcase of the stars for the fans. It was played for bragging rights between the American and National League, no more and no less. Over a period of time the game seemed to lose some of its lusters. Perhaps it was because it was basically meaningless, or maybe because most people were on vacation, I don't know.

The league has done a lot of work to make the game something that the fans want to watch as well as take a bigger interest in, mostly a sign of the financial times since networks had committed a pile of money to broadcast the game. And of course the host team invests a significant amount of resources into showing their city off.

For decades the participants were selected by the players themselves, then in 2002 the league chose to have the fans make the final roster selections, since it is the fans paying to watch it. That has had its share of pros and cons as well, since often times star players will be elected over players having tremendous years, but no situation is perfect, I suppose.

They've even gone to the point of having the winner of the All-Star game determine who has home field advantage in the World Series! That has recently been changed. It should be the best team with the best record over 162 game that actually gets the home field advantage.

The All-Star game has had its twist an turns off the field, and it's also had just as many on the field. Let's look at some.

Babe Ruth

George Herman "Babe" Ruth is arguably the one name even the most casual fan associates with baseball. He played fourteen years for the New York Yankees, perhaps the most storied franchise in baseball.

What many don't know is that his career began in Boston, and that the cash-starved Red Sox actually sold his contract to New York. The rest, as they say, is history.

The inaugural All-Star game was played in 1933, when Babe Ruth was in the twilight of his career. The "Bambino," as he was often referred to, gave the fans what they came to see. In the bottom of the second inning he launched the first home run in All-Star game history, cementing his place as perhaps the greatest hitter ever.

Ray Fosse

The year was 1970 and the game was played in Cincinnati. Ray Fosse was a good player, but far from a perennial All-Star. As a catcher for the Cleveland Indians, he was having perhaps the best season of his career and voted to play in the All-Star game. Back then, the game was still a showcase of talent and the desire for players to actually win the game was relatively low. However, there was Pete Rose, or as we mentioned in Chapter One, "Charlie Hustle." Pete did play every game to win!

Attempting to score, he famously plowed into Ray Fosse at the plate, separating Fosse's shoulder, something Ray never fully recovered from. Although Fosse had a rather unremarkable career, he did play on two World Series winning teams, was an original member of the Seattle Mariners, and today is a broadcaster for the Oakland Athletics.

Bo Jackson

Bo is most known for his accomplishments on the football field, winning the Heisman Trophy as the best player in College Football in 1985. He was the first-overall draft pick of the Oakland Raiders, and spent several highly productive seasons playing in the National Football League.

Due to a severe hip injury, Bo was forced to retire from football. It was actually discovered that he had necrosis of the hip. That would force most people to become relatively sedate in life. Not Bo.

He had such drive that he chose to pursue a baseball career, most thought as a lark. But Bo did nothing for a lark, and in fact was so good he made the 1989 MLB All-Star game. The fans came out en masse to see Bo, and in an at-bat against Rick Reuschel, spanked a home run over the left-center field fence, giving the fans exactly what they came to see, and more.

John Kruk

John Kruk might be famous as a baseball analyst for ESPN. Well, he actually is. He is also a broadcaster for the Philadelphia Phillies, for whom he played over half of his career. Kruk was a bit of an anomaly, being one of only six players to retire with exactly 100 career home runs. He left the game with a lifetime .300 batting average, so John was no slouch.

In the 1993 All-Star game Kruk came to the plate to face future Hall of Fame pitcher Randy Johnson. Johnson threw harder than most anyone in that era, and on top of that had a very unconventional and intimidating throwing motion. Randy did at times have control problems.

In a very famous at-bat, Johnson, known as "The Big Unit" for his size, threw a pitch to Kruk that sailed about eight feet over his head, behind him, and it flew on the fly into the backstop! Kruk was so intimidated, he struck out swinging at the next two pitches looking like a scared little kid. He had literally backed out of the box to swing as the pitches were being delivered. So, for all the great and not-so-great plays, this moment will go down as clearly the most comical!

Johnson was so intimidating to left-handed hitters than in 1997's

All-Star game he made Larry Walker turn around and bat right handed. Larry actually drew a walk!

Al Rosen

Baseball players and athletes in general must have been tougher in the bygone era. Al Rosen was a third-baseman for the Cleveland Indians for a decade, and a great player. He was an American League MVP, a four-time All-Star, and won two home run titles.

I've often heard about how tough people from the Midwest were (although Al was born in South Carolina) and in 1954 Rosen proved just how competitive he was.

Remember, this is a game that at that time really meant very little in the grand scheme of things, but that year the game was played in Rosen's home stadium, Cleveland. He felt he had to play.

Rosen had broken a finger not long before the game, and in this day and age I have a hard time thinking a hangnail doesn't keep players from doing things they don't have to. Not only did Rosen play in the game, he smacked two home runs!

Emmett Ashford

We spent some time in Chapter One talking about Jackie Robinson, the first African American to play Major League Baseball. His accomplishment is so highly-regarded that every MLB team has retired his number, 42. Jackie broke the color barrier as a player in 1947.

But, it wasn't until 1967, a full two decades later, than an African American umpire would work an All-Star game.

Ashford left his job with the US Postal Service in 1951 to pursue his dream of being a Major League umpire. He'd held that job at the USPS for fifteen years, and ironically enough it would be exactly fifteen more years until he made his debut umpiring in the Major League.

He wasn't just any old umpire, either. Emmett was well-known for his showmanship and energy, and often even interacted with the fans in between innings.

What's even more interesting is that upon his death his ashes were brought to rest in Cooperstown, NY, the home of the MLB Hall of Fame.

Brian McCann

It's not very often that a baseball team, even a bad one, loses thirteen games in a row. Back in 1889 the Louisville Cardinals lost twenty-six straight games, but in modern-day baseball the odds of losing thirteen straight, especially a team comprised solely of All-Stars, is almost something you just can't calculate.

You would think that just by accident a team would not lose more than a few in a row, but for thirteen straight seasons the National League lost the All-Star game.

In 2010 the game was played in Anaheim, home of the Los Angeles

Angels. The backup NL catcher that year was Brian McCann of the Atlanta Braves, who after coming in to replace Yadier Molina, hit a bases-clearing, three-run double, for the NL's only runs of the game. Those three runs were enough to break an embarrassing streak, as they held on to win the game, 3-1.

The Year 2002

In regular season games, baseball teams usually have anywhere from five to eight pitchers in the bullpen. If need be, at times they'll even use a starting pitcher to come in and get one or two outs.

In an All-Star game it's become common practice for managers to put everyone in the game at some point, and in fact that's become one of the most controversial issues leading up to a game. Teams want to know how the managers will handle the pitching staff. Remember, these guys are on a strict routine during the season.

So, of course there's a new pitcher almost every inning, sometimes more often. In 2002 the game was tied after eleven innings. In the spirit of the game, and with no pitchers available, they declared the game a tie. The fans are still booing in Milwaukee!

Satchel Paige

Paige played professional baseball for almost three decades, yet there are many casual fans that might have never heard of him. There are at least two reasons for that. The first reason is that his career began way back in 1926 with the Chattanooga Look Outs.

If you've never heard of them it's likely because they were part of the Negro League, which existed up until 1951. After Jackie Robinson broke the color barrier in 1947, gradually teams accepted the fact that African Americans were equally as talented, and many teams went in search of them in the Negro Leagues.

Paige was one such talent, but by that time he was getting up in years, but still a very good pitcher. He was brought up by the Cleveland Indians, and in 1953 was with the St. Louis Browns. He was having such a tremendous season they voted him into the All-State game, so it was that year that at the age of 47 he became what is still the oldest player ever to appear in the All-Star game.

Dizzy Dean

Jay Hanna Dean was commonly referred to as "Dizzy," in part because of his colorful personality. As a pitcher for the Cardinals and Cubs, he had what's by some standards a relatively short career.

In his ten years in professional baseball, he was a World Series champion and a National League Most Valuable player. Additionally he led the league in strikeouts four times, consecutively. Those accomplishments were more than enough to get him elected into the Hall of Fame.

His career might not have been cut short if he weren't so good! In the 1937 All-Star game he was hit in the foot by a line drive, fracturing it. We talked about toughness earlier, and here's another example. Rather than properly let his foot heal, he went right back into action and was never quite the same pitcher again.

Reggie Jackson

Reggie was perhaps one of the most flamboyant players ever, starting his career with the Oakland A's, and playing five seasons with the Yankees. And of course in New York you're just going to be made bigger than life by the media. That has proven to a bad thing for those that couldn't handle the pressure, but not Reggie.

He ended up hitting 563 career home runs, which might have been even more in this day and age of "juiced" baseballs! That still ranks 14th on all-time list for career home runs.

Most home runs "do damage" to the other team. In 1971 Reggie hit a home run in the All-Star game off of Pirates pitcher Dock Ellis. In and of itself that seems like a regular feat. But this one not only went out of the park, but "did damage" to a transformer controlling the lights in Tiger Stadium. The ball is estimated to have traveled 530' and is listed as the longest home run ever hit in an All-Star game!

Rod Carew

Carew played most of his career when I was a young lad, and his baseball card is probably one of the ones I ruined in my bicycle spokes. To this day he's not in many discussions as perhaps one of the purest hitters in the game, but he was. He won seven batting titles and was an eighteen time MLB All-Star.

The fans like to see home runs, the big play, the big strikeout. Well, that wasn't Rod Carew. He amassed over 3000 hits in his career, and to put that in perspective there have been only 29 other players to reach that milestone. Ever.

But, only 92 of his hits were home runs.

Hitting home runs is easier to do than getting a triple. In the 1978 All-Star game Rod Carew actually lead off the game with a triple. In his next at-bat he did it again, becoming the first player in the history of the All-Star game to hit two triples, and it hasn't been done since.

Carew is still in the game as a batting instructor. In 2016 he was told he needed a heart transplant, and he received one - from Baltimore Ravens TE Konrad Reuland. This misfortune of Konrad suffering a brain aneurism at such a young age is keeping Rod Carew "in the game."

Cal Ripken

Yes, for this we've got to put him on another list. For someone that set the record for most consecutive games played, and won numerous other awards, Ripken always preferred to stay out of the limelight. In fact, here's another true story. When I was a kid I made a habit of sending different players their baseball card with a SASE to see if I could get it autographed. Many did, many did not.

But, Cal took forever and ever and eventually I gave up.

Then, months later, lo and behold I get a letter from Baltimore with not only his card signed, but a handwritten letter, apologizing for taking so long. That just doesn't happen anymore.

In the 2001 All-Star game, which was near the end of his career, he was named to the team as a third baseman. He'd switched to that position because it requires less range. Before the first pitch, Alex Rodriguez, who had been elected to play shortstop, insisted on switching positions with Ripken, out of massive respect. Reluctantly Cal gave in, and there was a lengthy standing ovation from the fans and both dugouts. But, that wasn't enough. In the bottom of the third inning and in his first at-bat, he deposited the first pitch he saw over the fence for a home run!

Willie Mays

Not many baseball lists of all-time greats would omit Willie Mays. Dubbed "The Say Hey Kid" by the press, Mays was on the roster of twenty-one All-Star teams and played in twenty-four All-Star games. You may be asking how he can have 24 games and be on 21 rosters!

Well, for several years there were two All-Star games per season. That longevity is surpassed only by Hank Aaron, who we're saving for a special moment in another chapter.

There are only four players in baseball history that have whacked more balls over the fence than Mays, and he also won 12 Golden

Glove awards as the premier defensive center-fielder in the league.

When it comes to All-Star games, Mays has some records that may stand forever. One is that he has 82 All-Start plate appearances, and with the specialization and the need to get every player in the game, that will likely not be broken. He has 40 total bases (the equivalent of 10 home runs) and has scored 20 runs. Those numbers alone would be enough to get him to Cooperstown. And yet, Willie missed almost two full seasons due to military service!

Roberto Clemente

Almost everyone that follows baseball and even many that don't have heard the name Roberto Clemente. Born in Puerto Rico, Clemente debuted for the Pittsburgh Pirates in 1955, and ended his career with exactly 3000 hits. Roberto was an All-Star fifteen times!

Aside from being one of the best players in the game, Clemente was also one of the most philanthropic players as well. Unfortunately that generosity is what contributed to his untimely death. In 1972 there had been a massive earthquake in Nicaragua, and when Clemente learned that much of the relief supplies were being diverted by corrupt government officials, he decided that perhaps his presence might help the supplies reach the intended victims. However, on New Year's Eve of that year, his plane, which was overloaded by some two tons, crashed into the Atlantic Ocean and took his life. The Roberto Clemente Award is now given to the MLB player each season that shows the most sportsmanship and kindness, and has become one of the most coveted awards by the players.

Clemente holds so many All-Star records we couldn't fit them all on one page. But the one he owns that sets him apart from everyone is the fact that he's the only player to strike out four times in one game!

RANDOM FUN FACTS

1. The official attendance for the 1999 All-Star game at Fenway Park was 34,187. That was actually a few thousand less than attended the Midsummer Classic in Boston in 1946!

2. The very first All-Star game was in 1933 at Comiskey Park in Chicago, home of the White Sox. The attendance for the inaugural game was 49,200, and was actually held as part of the World's Fair.

3. To gain entry into the first All-Star game in 1933 a fan had to cough up $1.65, tax included. A ticket to the Home Run Derby in 2017 can cost as much as $1910 on the secondary market.

4. A switch-hitter will bat from both sides of the plate, depending on whether it's a left or right-handed pitcher. There have been 306 times a player has hit a home run from both sides of the plate in the same game.

5. Mickey Mantle hit a home run from both sides of the plate eight times in the game. Twice in one year! To put that in perspective, he's done it 2.6% of the times it's ever been done.

6. The first time a baseball game was played indoors was in the Houston Astrodome in 1965. I grew up in Boston attending games in Fenway Park and still can't comprehend that.

7. The longest game ever played in professional baseball was in 1981. It was in AAA game between the Pawtucket Red Sox and the Rochester Red Wings. The Red Sox won, 3-2, in about 8.5 hours.

8. A no-hitter, where a pitcher throws an entire game without giving up a hit, is very rare. Johnny Vander Meer did it twice in 1938. Consecutively.

9. The Philadelphia Phillies have been around since 1883 and have lost over 10,700 games in their history. Typically the worst team in baseball loses about 100 games in a given season, so that would translate into being the worst team in MLB for about 107 years straight.

10. In September of 1896 the Louisville Cardinals lost all three games of a tripleheader. The next day they lost both games of a doubleheader. So, they are the only team in history to lose five games in two days.

11. In 1993 the Colorado Rockies set the single-season attendance record, drawing just under 4,500,000 fans for their home games.

12. The Red Sox and the Dodgers played an exhibition game in the Los Angeles Memorial Coliseum in 2008 that drew over 115,000 fans. That's almost 10,000 more fans than were at the most-attended Rose Bowl, ever, in 1973.

13. Each side of a base in 15" long and the official rules state that

each base must be secured to the ground.

14. Jimmy Piersall hit 104 home runs over the course of his career. When he hit his 100th, he ran the bases backwards.

15. Don Baylor played in the World Series three different times. Many players never get to play in one, let alone three. Don had the distinction of doing it three straight years, with three different teams.

16. Turning a triple play is probably the rarest feat in baseball. On average it happens four or five times in a season. In 1990 the Minnesota Twins did it twice. In the same game.

17. The New York Yankees were the first team to wear numbers on their backs.

18. The "Star Spangled Banner" was performed at a sporting event for the first time in 1918. It was in the middle of the 7th inning of a World Series game between the Cubs and the Red Sox.

19. The first professional game ever aired on television was a between Brooklyn and Cincinnati in 1939.

20. Dock Ellis threw his first and only no-hitter in 1970. Rumor, which Dock has never denied, is that he was high on LSD at the time.

TEST YOURSELF – QUESTIONS AND ANSWERS

1. Who is the only player to hit two triples in an MLB All-Star game?

   A. Ty Cobb

   B. Willie Mays

   C. Rod Carew

2. Who was the first African American umpire to work an All-Star game?

   A. Al Rosen

   B. Satchel Paige

   C. Emmett Ashford

3. Who is credited with having hit the longest home run in All-Star history?

   A. Babe Ruth

   B. Brian McCann

   C. Reggie Jackson

4. What pitcher threw two no-hitters in consecutive games?

   A. Dizzy Dean

   B. Johnny Vander Meer

C. Al Rosen

5. Which player has the record for most career All-Star at bats?

   A. Cal Ripken

   B. Willie Mays

   C. Bo Jackson

ANSWERS

1. C
2. C
3. C
4. B
5. B

CHAPTER THREE:
THE WORLD SERIES

We just finished the chapter on the Midsummer Classic, now we're devoting a chapter entirely to the Fall Classic, or better known as the World Series. It's the pinnacle of sport, and teams play 162 regular season games just for the right to make the playoffs, let alone compete in the World Series. It's typically high drama, because it follows a month of Spring Training, six months of the regular season, and almost a month of playoff games.

Because of what's at stake, and probably more importantly the attention the World Series gets on television, every pitch of every inning and every at-bat seems to be magnified. The networks have paid millions and millions of dollars for the right to broadcast it. MLB's deal with Fox Sports and ESPN signed in 2012 was reportedly and eight-year deal worth $12.4 billion. So, it's probably true that during the playoffs the network executives are quietly rooting against the smaller market teams. They'll be much happier and much fatter if a team from New York is playing a team from Los Angeles, as opposed to, well, Seattle and San Diego. Heck, San Diego can't keep an NFL franchise and that's not easy to do.

The players certainly don't care whether people are watching or not, and it's quite the show with some very memorable moments, both good and bad, depending on who you're rooting for! Being a lifelong Red Sox fan, I've been on both sides several times. Many times over the years, it's not the big names you've come to know that are the heroes (or goats), but often it's journeyman players, coaches, and managers, that are just in the right place at the right time.

Let's take a look at some of the more memorable moments and games, starting with one that might be painful for some Boston fans.

Bill Buckner

The year was 1986 and the teams were the Boston Red Sox and the New York Mets. Buckner had spent most of his illustrious career with the Chicago Cubs, and since his knees were shot he was relegated to playing first base, perhaps the position on the field that requires the least movement. Although Boston fans may disagree with lack of movement required.

Bill could still hit, though. In game six at Shea Stadium, the Red Sox had a 3-2 lead in games In what is a best of seven series. So, win this game and erase almost 100 years of futility in Boston.

The game was tied and went into extra innings. Boston scored two runs in the top of the 10th inning to take a 5-3 lead. Boston was really about to do it! Then came the bottom of the 10th, and with two outs and two runners on base, Mookie Wilson hit a slow rolling ground ball right to Buckner at first base. There it was. The game was going to be over! However, in what can only be described as one of the most egregious errors in the history of baseball, the ball inconceivably rolled through his legs and into right field, and the Mets walked off 6-5 winners. They won game seven and the World Series.

In Boston, right behind Pearl Harbor, that's "the day that will live in infamy."

Kirk Gibson

Gibson was one of the better players on the Detroit Tigers for years, and this was back when men were men. You just didn't rest or sit out unless there was something life-threatening going on.

In 1988 an arbitrator ruled that there had been collusion amongst some of the owners and granted several players immediate free agency, among them was Kirk Gibson.

Gibson signed to play with the Los Angeles Dodgers. That year Los Angeles made it to the World Series, playing against the Oakland A's.

In the NLCS Gibson injured both legs and wasn't expected to play in the World Series. The guy could hardly walk. With the Dodgers trailing by a run in the bottom of the ninth and a runner on, Gibson was put in to pinch hit. It was all or nothing, because the guy simply wasn't going to run, period. As fate would have it, Gibson launched one of the most famous home runs in World Series history. He hobbled around the bases and the Dodgers would go on to win the World Series.

Reggie Jackson

Reggie was known for a lot of accomplishments and as we alluded to earlier, the longest home run in All-Star history. That was one moment of many, and many of those moments came in post-season play, hence he was often referred to as "Mr. October."

In the 1977 World Series, Reggie hit not one, not two, but three home runs off of three different Dodger pitchers. There have been several players to hit three home runs in a World Series, but what Reggie did that year can only be duplicated, never surpassed.

He hit all three of them on the first pitch he saw!

Reggie was a 14-time All-Star, league MVP, won the World Series five times, and four times he was the American League home run champion. But, it's what he did when it really mattered that this first-ballot Hall of Famer will be most remembered for.

Curt Shilling

Schilling had a lengthy career with several teams. He began his career with Baltimore in 1988 and ended it with the Red Sox in 2007.

He was a six-time All-Star and was on the winning World Series team three times. In fact, he was a winner of the prestigious Roberto Clemente award.

Perhaps his most famous moment came in 2004, the year Boston won the World Series for the first time in over eight decades. He had developed some very serious ankle tendon issues and had some quick procedures done, enough so that with the procedures and a few injections, he could pitch.

In one of the games his ankle was such a mess that he was literally bleeding through his white sock. He gutted out a win, and for obvious reasons the game became known as "The Bloody Sock" incident.

One of the socks was sold at auction in 2013 for $92,613!

Don Larsen

Throwing a no-hitter is quite the accomplishment, and perhaps once or twice in an entire season it does happen. A no-hitter is still referred to as no-hitter if a pitcher walks someone, or there's an error. As long as there are not hits, it's a no-hitter.

In 1956 Don Larsen took that one step further. Not only did he not allow a walk, nor was there an error in the field, but he faced and retired all 27 batters he faced, throwing what's known as a "perfect game."

He had a rather unremarkable career, playing for eight teams over 14 years, and in fact lost more games than he won. However, on that day he did something that's only been done 23 times in the history of baseball, and that's the one and only time it's been done in the World Series!

Bill Mazeroski

Mazeroski played second base for the Pittsburgh Pirates from 1956-1972, or his entire 17-year career. Bill was known more for his defensive prowess and in fact holds the record for most double plays by a second-baseman.

He did amass over 2000 hits in his career, and spanked 138 home runs. To put those home runs in perspective, many players today hit that many in three seasons.

But in 1960 the unlikely slugger hit a home run that the Pirates and many baseball fans will never forget. In the bottom of the ninth inning of game seven, a moment that doesn't get any bigger in baseball, Mazeroski hit the game and World Series winning home run off of Yankees pitcher Ralph Terry.

A 14-year-old fan retrieved the ball and actually had it signed by Bill. The ball was later lost when the kid used in a game. That ball would have fetched a couple of dollars at an auction, or at the very least be in the Hall of Fame!

Carlton Fisk

Fisk was a long-time catcher in the American League, playing about half his career in Boston and the remainder for the White Sox. In the 1975 World Series he was involved in two incidents that'll never be forgotten.

In the third of the series, against the Cincinnati Reds, Fisk was behind the plate. Ed Armbrister tried to lay down a bunt. Armbrister made it very difficult for Fisk to get to the ball, and whether it was intentional or not may never be known. The umpire failed to call interference, Fisk threw wildly, and the Reds won the game.

In the sixth game of the series, Fisk hit what is still one of the most memorable home runs in all of baseball history, not just the World Series. In the 12th inning, Fisk connected with one that was going to be clearly long enough to clear the fence. The only question was whether or not it would stay fair. The image of Fisk heading in the direction of first base waving his arms in an effort to perhaps effect the wind and keep it fair is one that's still shown regularly on World Series promos by television networks.

The ball hit the foul pole, which is considered fair territory, and Boston won the game. They did lose game seven and the World Series, however.

Loma Prieta Earthquake

This is about an incident, not a player, but it's one of the most memorable moments in World Series history. In 1989 the Oakland Athletics and the San Francisco Giants were set to play the third game of the series on October 17th.

ABC was carrying the game, which was only moments away from the first pitch. The commentators were Al Michaels, who many may know was also the broadcaster who called the US Ice Hockey team win over Russia in the 1980 Olympics. In the booth with Michaels was long-time Cardinals catcher and long-time (and still) broadcaster Tim McCarver.

With the world watching and 62,000 people in their seats, all of a sudden you heard Al exclaim "I'll tell you what, we're having an earth------". And then the broadcast signal was lost!

Don Denkinger

As we just saw, it's not always the players that have impacts on or are involved in big moments. Sometimes its nature, and sometimes it's the umpire!

In the 1985 World Series between the Kansas City Royals and the St. Louis Cardinals, it was the 8th inning of the sixth game. Jorge Orta hit a slow ground ball up the first base side, which was fielded by the first basemen, who tossed it to the pitcher covering the base. Denkinger called Orta safe.

It was clear even to the naked eye he was out, and television replay showed that he was indeed out, by as much as half-a-step! Unfortunately, that was long before replay was involved, so the call stood. After the game Denkinger said he was listening for the sound of the ball hitting the glove, which is actually quite common. But, he said, the crowd noise was too loud!

He received hate mail and death threats, and in fact two St. Louis radio personalities went so far as to give out his phone number and home address. The even bigger irony is that he was scheduled to be the home plate umpire in the next game.

Scott Posednik

Often times, and actually more often than not, a World Series hero is someone that's in the right place at the right time and does that thing everyone remembers. It's not always the Babe Ruths' or names people know off the tip of their tongue.

If there was ever a "journeyman" it was Posednik. He played 11 years In the baseball for seven different teams. If they'd have had frequent flyer miles back then he'd have owned his own airline.

In 2005 Scott and his White Sox were in the World Series. In the second game, tied at 6, it was Posednik's turn at the plate. He promptly launched a walk-off home run into the stands, which alone doesn't sound like much. But, it was only the 14th time in World Series history a game had ended with a home run.

What's more improbable is that Scott hit exactly zero home runs during that regular season!

Gil Hodges - Shoe Polish

Hodges was both a player and a manager in baseball for almost three decades. As a player he was an eight-time All-Star and played on three World Series champion winning teams. By 1969 his career as a player was over, and he was the manager of the New York Mets, facing the heavily favored Baltimore Orioles in the World Series.

In the fifth game of the series, Orioles pitcher Dave McNally hit Cleon Jones on the foot with a pitch. However, home plate umpire Lou DiMuro called it a ball, ruling that it didn't hit Jones.

Hodges came out of the dugout to argue the call, as most managers would. But Hodges had the evidence! He showed DiMuro the ball, which had black shoe polish on it from hitting Jones' cleats. DiMuro subsequently reversed the call, something you just don't see these days.

Even more ironic, the next batter, Donn Clendenon, hit a two run home run.

Derek Jeter

Jeter played twenty seasons for the New York Yankees and did so many things in his career we could write an entire book on Jeter alone. For starters, and what's most impressive in this day and age, is that he played his entire career for one team.

He was on five Yankee teams that won the World Series, was a 14-time All-Star, won the Roberto Clemente award, and five times was voted the best defensive shortstop in the American League.

In 2001 he launched the game winning home run in extra innings to win the fourth game of the World Series for New York. I suppose he hit the game winning home runs plenty of times. However, MLB was in the age where television dictated much of the schedule, and by now we were playing later and later in October. This particular game was played on the last day of the October, and because it was a long game, that home run occurred shortly after midnight, making it technically November 1st.

Because New York already had a Mr. October, Reggie Jackson, Jeter was promptly dubbed "Mr. November."

Edgar Renteria

Renteria played 15 seasons of Major League baseball, mostly unremarkable. I suppose given the odds of playing for that many years, It is remarkable. But Edgar wasn't an elite player, just a very good one who could play many different positions.

Renteria spent the first three years of his career with the Florida Marlins, at the time an expansion team. In 1997 Florida (now the Miami Marlins) made it all the way to the World Series.

That was also several years after baseball added a "Wild Card" team to the playoffs in an effort to keep more teams viable longer into the season. Florida made the playoffs as a Wild Card team, not by winning their division.

That year Renteria was a mere 20 years old. He came up to the plate in the 11th inning of the decisive Game Seven, with the bases loaded. He singled up the middle off of Cleveland pitcher Charles Nagy to give Florida the World Series title, making them the first-ever Wild Card team to win a World Series, and in only their fifth year of existence.

David Freese

Freese came into the league in 2009 and is still currently playing in the Pittsburgh Pirates organization. He made the All-Star team in 2012 for the first time, and is yet another in a long line of World Series heroes who might fall into the "unlikely" category.

The year was 2011 and Freese was with the St. Louis Cardinals, who were in the World Series that year, playing the Texas Rangers. They found themselves behind three games to two, and trailing game six 7-5. It appeared Texas was going to be the World Series winners.

In the bottom of the ninth, up strolled Freese, with Albert Pujols on second base, and two outs. Of course we know what he did next, which was hit a game tying, two-run triple. But, it's what he did next that really makes it special.

In the bottom of the 11th he led off the inning with a game-winning home run! The Cardinals would go on to win the next game, and obviously the World Series.

Willie Mays

Yes, Willie, again. Like so many before him in this book, once is not enough. We've already documented his accomplishments, but there's more. And of course it happened in a World Series game.

The year was 1954, and it was the first game of the World Seris against the Cleveland Indians. In the bottom of the ninth inning, the game tied at two, Indians slugger Vic Wertz drove a ball deep (and I mean deep) to centerfield that appeared would easily drive home the two base runners.

But, Willie tracked it all the way to the warning track, and in a dead sprint the ball dropped harmlessly into his glove. It's probably "the" Willie Mays defensive highlight of his career, still shown repeatedly on television. It's known simply as "The Catch."

The Giants went on to win the game in extra innings, and in fact won all four games to sweep the series.

RANDOM FUN FACTS

1. "Take Me Out to the Ballgame" was written in 1908 by two people who had never been to a baseball game.

2. Only six of the parks in use today were built before 1989, the oldest being Fenway Park, built in 1912.

3. In an average nine-inning game, teams go through approximately 70 baseballs.

4. Baseball has seen growth for thirteen straight years, with revenues in 2016 at a robust $9.5 billion.

5. The legendary Mickey Mantle holds the record for the longest home run ever hit, 565'. He did that in Griffith Stadium in Washington in 1953.

6. Rick Monday, at the time playing for the Chicago Cubs, saved an American flag. During a game at Dodger Stadium in 1976, two men were in the outfield trying to burn it.

7. Barry Bonds has won the Most Valuable Player award seven times. Nobody else has won the award more than three times.

8. Miguel Cabrera won the Triple Crown in 2012, leading the league in home runs, batting average, and runs batted in. It hadn't been done since Carl Yastrzemski did it in 1967.

9. Frank Robinson won the Triple Crown only the year prior, in 1966.

10. Vida Blue of the Oakland Athletics was the youngest player to ever win the Most Valuable Player award. He did so in 1971, and when the season began he was 21 years old.

11. There have been three players that have "hit for the cycle" in both the National and American Leagues. Michael Cuddyer did it most recently, preceded by John Olerud and Bob Watson.

12. Everyone has heard of Yogi Berra, but few know that in 1950 he only struck out 12 times in 656 at bats. That equales to about one every other week!

13. In 2009, Mark Reynolds struck out 223 times. That's the record for a single season. By one.

14. In 1879 the Providence Grays were the first professional baseball team to install netting behind home plate.

15. The fastest baseball game ever played occurred in 1919 and lasted fifty-one minutes. I do not know the exact amount, but there are probably fifty-one minutes of commercials today.

16. On July 19, 1982, future Hall of Famer Tony Gwynn recorded his first hit. On July 19, 2006, his son (Tony Gwynn, Jr.) recorded his first hit.

17. Bob Feller once struck out seventeen batters in a game. He was seventeen years old.

18. A lot of pitchers develop a knuckle-ball, which is less stressful on the body. Some do so in an attempt to lengthen their

careers. Phil Niekro was so successful with it he won more game in his 40's than he did in his 30's.

19. Long-time Oakland A's relief pitcher Rollie Fingers is in the Hall of Fame, with more losses than wins.

20. The San Diego Padres have been in existence since 1969. They are the only team that hasn't thrown a no-hitter.

TEST YOURSELF – QUESTIONS AND ANSWERS

1. What umpire changed his call from a ball to a HBP after seeing shoe polish on the ball?

    A. Emmett Ashford
    B. Lou DiMuro
    C. Don Denkinger

2. Who is the only pitcher to throw a perfect game in the World Series?

    A. Don Larsen
    B. Cy Young
    C. Dave McNally

3. What two teams were playing in the World Series when the Loma Preita earthquake interrupted it?

    A. Boston Red Sox/Los Angeles Dodgers
    B. San Francisco Giants/Oakland A's
    C. Los Angeles Angels/Colorado Rockies

4. Whose only hit in the 1988 World Series was a pinch-hit home run?

    A. Carlton Fisk

B. Edgar Renteria

C. Kirk Gibson

5. Who made what's now referred to as "The Catch" off the bat of Vic Wertz?

A. Kirby Puckett

B. Willie Mays

C. Reggie Jackson

ANSWERS

1. B
2. A
3. B
4. C
5. B

CHAPTER FOUR:

FRANCHISES/BALL PARKS

Some ball parks used today were being used over 100 years ago, while many more are quite modern, with retractable roofs, and cost 100's of millions of dollars to construct. Some of the stadiums still sit where they did 100 years ago, and some are barely 50 years old. It's my guess that when Abner Doubleday invented the game (if in fact he did!) that he hardly could imagine ordering a steak from your seat and charging it to a credit card!

But, that's becoming the rule rather than the exception as many fans are in attendance these days for the experience as much as the game itself. And, as the cost of doing business goes up every year, teams must find new revenue streams. Some of them are quite creative, while others just keep raising prices.

And the teams that play the game have changed. Yes, the Cubs are still the Cubs. But, many franchises either folded for lack of funds, or simply moved to another town where it might be more profitable. Years ago, that was a relatively easy process. These days, to move a sports franchise almost takes an act of congress, and certainly the fans pay for it one way or another. If the team stays in town, they usually build a new stadium, and more often than not using municipal bonds that the fans have to fund, in some form or fashion.

So, the old, the new, and the in-between. They've all got their nuances and special places in history.

Chicago Cubs/Wrigley Field

From 1920 through 1926 the park was simply called Cubs Park. William Wrigley (yes, the chewing gum Wrigley) acquired control of the team in 1921. It's the oldest park in the league, built in 1914, and was actually known then as Weeghman Park. Charles Weeghman had it built as the owner of the Chicago Wales, but apparently he wasn't the businessman Wrigley was.

The Cubs and Wrigley actually forced baseball to make a contingency plan for the World Series in 1984. The Cubs were in the NLCS, and if they'd have beaten the Padres (they did not), Wrigley Field still didn't have lights yet. And of course by then television pretty much dictated policy as to when the games would be played, and almost always at night.

The field was nicknamed "The Friendly Confines," a phrase we hear thrown around loosely quite often. It is credited to Ernie Banks, a long-time Cubs third baseman many call "Mr. Cub."

Most know the Cubs won a World Series in 1908, and didn't win another one for 108 years, as in 2016 they beat the Cleveland Indians to win it all.

Toronto Blue Jays/Rogers Centre

The Chicago Cubs hadn't won a World Series in 69 years, and in 1977 MLB awarded a franchise to Toronto, and the Toronto Blue Jays actually won two titles before the Cubs did in 2016! They were originally owned by Labatt's Brewing Company, and are now majority owned by Rogers Communication.

I suppose Rogers Communications is doing well for themselves, since the stadium is named, aptly, Rogers Centre. This is as opposed to selling naming rights, which many teams do almost out of financial necessity. Rogers Centre (formerly The Sky Dome) opened for baseball in June of 1989 with a construction cost of just under $600 million, and has a retractable roof, one of the first of its kind. I can certainly understand the need for the roof, as April temperatures in Toronto are not always conducive to outdoor sports.

As an expansion team in 1989 Forbes valued them at $150 million. By the year 2012 their value had tripled, or somewhere in the neighborhood of $500 million. Today, Forbes values the Toronto Blue Jays at $1.3 billion!

Tampa Bay Rays/Tropicana Field

For over thirty years the Tampa/St.Petersburg area tried unsuccessfully to get a baseball franchise. Finally, in 1995 The Tampa Bay Devil Rays were born. The nickname "Devil Rays" came about as a reference to a manta ray and the sun, naturally. But, in

1997 and in the spirit of being politically correct, they were simply called the Rays.

That first decade was perhaps one of the most futile for any MLB franchise, even an expansion team. They finished in last place in the AL East nine of ten years. It didn't help that they were in the same division as the Red Sox and Yankees, but you'd think by accident they'd improve over that period of time.

Although they've yet to win a World Series, they did win an AL pennant in 2008.

You'd think a team in Central Florida wouldn't need a dome, but that's what they've got. Tropicana Field, known as "The Trop," doesn't have a retractable roof of any sort, it opened in 1990 and was known as The Suncoast Dome, then the Thunderdome, now The Trop.

On the field there's a real downside to playing in a climate-controlled dome, that's if you're a fan of scoring and home runs. There's very little air flow so the ball doesn't carry nearly as well as they do in the open air. For that reason, The Trop has always been a great place to pitch and typically has much lower scoring games than most venues.

Prior to them being competitive, they did bring along some talent, but as a small market team struggling to draw fans, they couldn't afford to keep players in Tampa Bay, so there's a ton of ex-Rays players doing quite well for themselves around the league.

Washington Nationals/Nationals Park

Washington had a baseball team long before the Nationals. They had the Senators from 1901-1960, and were one of the American League's eight original franchises. In 1960, after almost moving to several other cities, the Nationals (as they had become known) moved to Minneapolis and are what we now know as the Minnesota Twins!

They soon created a Minor League team in DC, known of course as the Senators. The team we know as the Nationals today was at one time, The Montreal Expos. The Expos were the first non-US based team, and they were reasonably competitive off and on. But, after a work stoppage in 1994, the Expos were forced to sell off most of their young talent, the losses started stacking up, and the cash flow was negative. Off they went to Washington.

Nationals Park is the first LEED (Leadership in Energy and Environmental Design) certified "green" sports stadium in the United States.

Since relocating, the Washington Nationals have won three NL East Division titles, but have yet to make it to the World Series. I suspect some in Congress will find a way to make that happen sooner rather than later.

New York Yankees/Yankee Stadium

No list can leave this team or that stadium off, but "that" stadium is not the original Yankee Stadium. The original Yankee Stadium, which opened in 1923, was demolished over time, finally completely gone in May of 2010. The original Yankee Stadium hosted 6581 baseball games, and because the Yankees were perennial winners, 161 post-season games, more than any other baseball stadium. Probably more than any ten other ball parks.

What's arguably one of baseball's most cherished moments, and perhaps the most memorable moment in the old Yankee Stadium, occurred on July 4, 1939. It was the day Lou Gehrig gave his farewell speech, calling himself "the luckiest man on earth." In a previous chapter we talked about Gehrig's longevity and consecutive game streak. He was diagnosed with a debilitating disease that today we refer to simply as ALS, or, Lou Gehrig's disease.

Babe Ruth hit the first home run in the old park in 1923. He said after the game:

> "I was glad to have hit the first home run in this park. God only knows who will hit the last"

In 2008 that honor fell to Jose Molina, the Yankees catcher from 2007-09.

There are entirely too many superlatives only one paragraph or two about this team. The long and short of it is that they've won the World Series 27 times, and won the American League pennant 40 times.

Seattle Mariners/Safeco Field

When people think of "mariners" they tend to think of older ones, like the ancient ones. Perhaps like the Vikings. But the Mariners haven't been around that long! They were born in 1977 and have yet to win a pennant, although they've been to the playoffs four times. Still, that's somewhat of an under achievement for 40 years of existence. It's not for lack of trying. Or buying. They did trade away Alex Rodriguez way back when, but that was almost pre-revenue sharing and as a small market team they really had no choice. Since then, they have gone out and got/bought players, but they just haven't been able to execute to their potential.

A little-known fact is that they were born of a lawsuit. In 1970 the Seattle Pilots were purchased and relocated to what we now know as the Milwaukee Brewers. The State of Washington sued the American League for breach of contract. Certain that they would eventually prevail, the County took it upon themselves to build the Kingdome three years before the Mariners were born, and the Kingdome was also home to the Seattle Seahawks.

Like many teams, what we'd have considered a palace at one time (the Kingdome) became obsolete, so Safeco Field was opened in 1999, and as many new venues do, it has a retractable roof. So although the Mariners haven't done much on the field, there's plenty to talk about off the field.

Miami Marlins/Marlins Park

The team began play in 1993, and have yet to win a Division Title. However, they've won the World Series twice. They were the first team to win it as a Wild Card team in 1997, and duplicated that again in 2003. They've always been a tough sell to fans in South Florida, and in fact many pro sports franchises have struggled in Florida, mainly because most fans are from somewhere else and have their own lifetime affiliation with other teams.

It looks as if the Marlins are going to be sold in 2017, and that's probably a good thing for both Miami and baseball. Their current owner, Jeffrey Loria, has been in and out of baseball and none of his attempts have succeeded. In fact, he was part of the now-defunct Montreal Expos, and several other Minor League and/or failed businesses. He's even involved in political goings on. He was recently rumored to have a handshake deal with Jared Kushner, Donald Trump's son-in-law, to buy the team. On the surface, that seems shady at the very least these days. But, it gets worse. The rumor was that Trumps' team was in the process of naming Loria the Ambassador to France!

Needless to say, there was plenty of controversy and accusation going around when the Marlins had Marlin Park built. It was finished in 2012 and allowed them to move out of the Miami Dolphins field, but there were relocation threats and all kinds of shady questions surrounding Lorie at the time. Now, since Kushner may not buy the team, it's possible that Derek Jeter and some other investors will, which can only be a good thing.

Atlanta Braves/SunTrust Field

SunTrust Field was just opened this season. Why they had to have a new stadium is beyond me, although I'm sure it's mainly financial and to draw fans. Their old stadium, Turner Field, was built in 1997 for the Centennial Olympic Games. I've been there, and having grown up in Fenway Park, Turner Field was like the Holy Grail to the me. It was in a rather difficult place in Atlanta to get to, but let's be realistic. What parks are easily accessible by multiple forms of transportation?

But, the Atlanta Braves as we know them today, have "only" been the Atlanta Braves since 1966. From 1953 through 1965 they were the Milwaukee Braves. So, the Milwaukee Braves move to Atlanta and the Seattle Pilots move to Milwaukee and are now the Brewers. Got it?

But, before the Milwaukee stint, they were in Boston. Yes, the Boston Braves, among other names. So they were in Boston from 1871 until 1952, so yes, for many years Boston had the Braves and the Red Sox.

Even after all those years, counting the ones in Boston, they've won exactly three World Series titles. Only one of those, in 1995, was in Atlanta. For many years they were one of the perennial contenders, but year after year, always a bridesmaid and never a bride. Well, once!

Colorado Rockies/Coors Field

Ahh, Coors Field. Well, it's quite clear why they call it Coors Field. You guys know this one. Coors Beer. Colorado-brewed with that fresh spring water. Well, that and Coors Brewing Company coughed up a fair bit of money for the naming rights. Coors Field is perhaps the smallest park in baseball, and add to that the thin air in the Mile High City, and scores there often approach what would be a low scoring football game! So much so that the Rockies have had a hard time attracting top-flight pitchers since they just know their stats are going to suffer. It's almost sad that it's come to that, but it is all about the money. Of course hitters would go play there for less money just to pad their stats for the bigger contract elsewhere.

The Rockies franchise is still in its infancy, only being born in 1993. However, they do have one National League pennant. Only four years after the franchise began, in 1996, Colorado made the playoffs as a Wild Card team and advanced to the Fall Classic. Sadly for them, they were swept in four straight games by the Boston Red Sox. But, by comparison, they're light years ahead of some franchises in term of relatively early success.

Only one player, Todd Helton, has had his number retired. Keli McGregor also does - he was a front office executive until his untimely death in 2010 at the age of 47. The third number they've got retired, and you should know this, is Jackie Robinson. The color barrier-breaker whose number has been retired by every team.

St. Louis Cardinals/Busch Stadium

It should be pretty clear why they call it Busch Stadium! But, it wasn't always just the Anheuser-Busch name. In 1953 it was named simply after Gussie Busch, obviously the brewing magnate, but since that time this is actually the third St. Louis venue to bear the name "Busch" Stadium. And yes, of course, Anheuser Busch paid a big fee for the naming rights.

This "Busch" Stadium opened in 2006, and what's funny is that the highest attendance ever to see a sporting event there is not a Cardinal game. Rather, it was a soccer match between Chelsea and Manchester.

Originally the franchise was known as the St. Louis Browns back in 1883.

They've won 11 World Series titles and 19 NL Pennants. The Cardinals signed a deal with Fox Sports Midwest in 2015 that doesn't take effect until 2018, which on the surface sounds benign. But, through the year 2032 the deal is worth $1 billion, with a "B."

New York Mets/Citi Field

When people hear "New York", they might assume the Mets have been around forever. But that would be the Yankees that have been around forever. The Mets were formed in 1962, originally playing at The Polo Grounds. They called Shea Stadium home for many years, and then in 2008 they built and opened Citi Field.

Clearly Citigroup Financial Services has something to do with that name! That and about $900 million and you've got yourself a ballpark.

They won their first World Series in 1969, and that year they were dubbed "The Micacle Mets," simply because they had been an exercise in futility for so many years. In fact, they famously passed on drafting Reggie Jackson in the amateur draft, instead taking Steve Chilcott. Chilcott never played in the Major Leagues. We know what Reggie did.

They won a second title in 1986, one famously gifted to them by the Red Sox.

One thing that's probably surprising to most people is that the Mets held the single-season New York attendance record for 29 years. They broke a record previously held by the Yankees since 1948, drawing 2.7 million fans in 1970.

Detroit Tigers/Comerica Park

Finally we get some stability on our list. The Tigers were formed in Detroit in 1901 and remain the same Tiger team today. Because of that, they are the oldest continuous one-name, one-city franchise in baseball.

They also have a longevity thing going on with their parks. In 1912 they moved into what was at the time called Navin Field. It had been expanded several times, and the name had changed from Navin Field to Briggs Stadium to Tiger Stadium. Then of course modernization was almost required to financially compete, and in 2000 Comerica Park was built, their current home.

What is surprising is in that all those years they've only won the World Series four times, the most recent coming back in 1984. Their lack of titles hasn't come from a lack of talent, as they've got a dozen players or managers in the Hall of Fame wearing Tiger caps, and another fourteen that played for the Tigers but are in the HOF with another cap. For the record, and barring the player being deceased, it's the players choice as to what uniform to wear in the Hall of Fame.

Boston Red Sox/Fenway Park

Watching a game at Fenway is on many bucket lists, and well it should be. It's the quintessential definition of "they just don't build 'em like that anymore." Built in 1912, it's the oldest park in baseball. It's the fourth smallest in terms of seating capacity, and second smallest in total capacity. Many of the newer parks have a lot of standing-room-only seats, hence the big discrepancy.

Fenway is most known for "The Green Monster," or the huge leftfield wall. The wall itself is located only 315' from home plate, but is 38' high. It's mentally played havoc with tons of right-handed hitters trying to pull the ball over it, and it's made opposing leftfielders look rather silly trying to play defense out there. It's so different that for decades the Red Sox only had three leftfielders. They would be Ted Williams, Carl Yastrzemski, and Jim Rice.

What's also interesting is that all three of them are in the Hall of Fame.

Their World Series drought was well-documented for years. They won a bunch of titles in the early 1900's, the last being in 1918. It took them until 2004 to win another one. Perhaps one of their biggest claims to fame occurred off the field, and isn't something to brag about, either. Red Sox owner Harry Freeze sold Babe Ruth to the rival New York Yankees. The rest is literally history!

Arizona Diamondbacks/Chase Field

Major League Baseball rewarded the Phoenix area with a baseball franchise in 1998, the Diamondbacks. They play in Chase Field, which was formerly known as Bank One Ballpark, and renamed in 2005 after Bank One merged with the JP Morgan & Chase company. So, as usual, it's all about the money. Chase Field is one of the smaller parks in baseball, not in terms of seating capacity but in terms of the distance to the outfield fences. It's obviously got a retractable roof, but it's rarely ever open. Most teams with retractable domes have it open when it's good weather. Well, it's almost always good weather in Arizona. It's just too hot! They don't ask the players and fans to enjoy or play a game when the temperatures are routinely above 110 degrees.

In 2001, in what was only their fourth year of existence, they won the World Series. They've got two retired jerseys already, if you don't count Jackie Robinson. They retired Randy Johnsons' jersey, a Hall of Fame pitcher, and Luis Gonzalez, a leftfielder. Gonzalez played many years in the league with many teams, but seven of those years with Arizona. His claim to fame is that he had the game-winning hit off of Yankees ace Mariano Rivera in the final game of 2001 World Series.

Minnesota Twins/Target Field

I you didn't know, you'd figure out as a baseball fan and trivia reader that the Target Corporation has its world headquarters in Minneapolis. With that said, Target Field didn't open until 2010. Before that, the Twins played in the Hubert H. Humprhey Metrodome. It was obviously a domed stadium, and had a fiberglass fabric roof that was self-supported by air pressure! Five different times a heavy snowfall caused the roof to collapse, and in 1982 only four days before the Minnesota Vikings were to play the Dallas Cowboys.

The Metrodome was one of the smaller parks, so many people started calling it the "Homer Dome," and to be honest I think most fans knew it more by that name that the HHH dome.

The Twins haven't always been in Minnesota. Well, the "Twins" have (aptly named after The Twin Cities of Minneapolis/St. Paul) but the franchise has not. We alluded to it earlier, but will do so one more time. Prior to 1961 the franchise was in Washington (DC) and known as the Senators.

They won the World Series in 1987 and again in 1991. They've got four legends in the Hall of Fame with Twins' caps on, and they would be Bert Blyleven, Harmon Killebrew, Rod Carew, and Kirby Puckett. The latter two we've referred to here on several occasions.

Perhaps the Twins biggest obstacle to the Twins winning more often is that small-market thing. They've often had very good players they either couldn't or chose not to pay. Perhaps the most famous of them was David Ortiz, who wound up being one of Boston's most revered players and will eventually be in the Hall of Fame.

RANDOM FUN FACTS

---

1. Hank Aaron and Babe Ruth ended their careers with exactly the same amount of runs scored, 2174.

2. Mike Schmidt holds the record for the most home runs for the Phillies at 548. The next closest to him (Ryan Howard) only has 311.

3. Speaking of the Phillies, back in 1971 Rise Wise threw a no-hitter. Pretty good in and of itself, but he also hit two home runs in that game.

4. David Cone is the only player to have won 20 games for both the New York Mets and the New York Yankees.

5. Victor Zambrano pitched for Tampa Bay in 2003 and not many hitters wanted to face him. It wasn't so much that he was that good, he was that wild. He threw 115 wild pitches that year and hit 20 batters.

6. Robby Thompson of the San Francisco Giants also holds a rather dubious record. He's the only player ever to get caught stealing four times in one game.

7. The shortest home run in history never left the infield, but you'll have to finish reading to find out who, what, and why.

8. Wade Boggs, of both Boston and the Yankees, ate chicken

before every game. During warm ups took exactly 150 ground balls.

9. Larry Walker of the Rockies must have liked the number 3. He set his alarm for 33 past the hour, and was married on November 3rd at 3.33 PM.

10. More Larry in three's! When he was in Montreal, he bought 33 tickets for disadvantaged children in Section 333.

11. Most players have superstitions. Pitcher Greg Swindell bit the top of one of his fingernails off and chewed in the entire time he was in the game.

12. Roger Clemens had an interesting pre-game routine. He had his trainer rub "the hottest possible substance" on his testicles. Really.

13. Back to Boggs. When Wade left Boston for the Evil Empire known as the Yankees, they won a World Series. Boston fans were already upset, but even more so when Wade was riding a horse around the warning track during the celebration.

14. Jason Giambi played many, many years in baseball and had many, many hitting slumps. His superstition to work out of them was to wear a golden thong. For what it's worth, Giambi hardly had six-pack abs.

15. Moises Alou had a rather unique way of avoiding calluses on his hands. He urinated on them. Apparently New York Yankee catcher Jorge Posada did the same thing.

16. I'm not sure MLB would allow it these days, but Craig Biggio of the Houston Astros never washed his batting helmet.

17. The average players uses one bat about every ten at-bats, which equates to 16,500 bats used in a season.

18. Although bats vary in price, the average is about $120. That means that there is about $1.98 million spent on baseball bats each year.

19. The "standard" MLB bat weighs about 32 ounces. It's said that Babe Ruth once used one weighing 54 ounces, and apparently modern-day slugger Bryce Harper is experimenting with one that weighs 47 ounces.

20. These days it's common for teams to draw more than three million fans in a season. The first year of recorded attendance was 1890 and the Philadelphia Phillies drew just over 148,000. That's three games for some teams today.

TEST YOURSELF – QUESTIONS AND ANSWERS

1. The Minnesota Twins have been in the Minneapolis/St. Paul area since 1961. Before that, they played in what city, as the Senators?

    A. St. Louis
    B. Boston
    C. Washington

2. The Washington Nationals of today were at one time an expansion team in what city?

    A. Seattle
    B. Toronto
    C. Montreal

3. The Atlanta Braves won the World Series in 1995 for the first time as the "Atlanta" Braves. Before moving to Atlanta, they were in what city?

    A. Boston
    B. Montreal
    C. Seattle

4. What long-time Chicago Cub great is simply known as Mr. Cub?

A. Ernie Banks

B. Ryne Sandberg

C. Willie Mays

5. What team was rumored to be being purchased by Donald Trumps' son-in-law, Jared Kushner?

A. Seattle Mariners

B. Miami Marlins

C. Tampa Bay Rays

ANSWERS

1. C
2. C
3. A
4. A
5. B

CHAPTER FIVE:

THE HALL OF FAME

Membership in the baseball Hall of Fame is an elite club, with only 317 members as of January of this year. That would include not only players, but managers, executives, umpires, and more. Let's assume we've had baseball for 130 years (which is being conservative), that would equate to only about 2.5 people per year making it to Cooperstown. If you figure the number of players alone that have come and gone, the overall odds for HOF induction might rival that of snow accumulating in Florida. Rare, to say the least.

Cooperstown was chosen for the site because it's where Abner Doubleday invented the game, and getting to Cooperstown is not easy. It's not like you fly into a big city and take a cab, by any means. In fact, Cooperstown is officially a village with a population of 1852 according to the latest census.

Cooperstown is about 100 miles from Syracuse about 75 miles from Albany, so yes, pretty much in the middle of nowhere.

There is much more to see at the Hall of Fame aside from the busts of some of the greats. There is memorabilia dating back to the before the turn of the century, and I don't mean the century that caused all the Y2K problems. I mean the turn of the century that was after the Civil War and before World War I.

So, if you can't get there, perhaps read on as we'll look inside the Hall of Fame. Many claim that it's merely a myth that Abner Doubleday created baseball, but whatever he did was in Cooperstown, so like it or not, that's what we're going with! We're going to look at some of the greats we haven't talked about yet.

Ernie Banks

Earlier I alluded to Ernie being called "Mr. Cub," but we didn't do him nearly enough justice. He was an African American, playing in an era of racial turmoil. Certainly less than Jackie Robinson, but it was still a time of tension and racial segregation. He came up through the Negro League and played as a teenager for one of the League's most famous teams, the Kansas City Monarchs.

He was, however, the first African American to play for the Chicago Cubs. The year was 1953, and it was late September, and Ernie was called up. The next year he started every game at shortstop for the Cubs. Shortstops are known far more for their defensive prowess, and Banks certainly was slick in the field. But, he also hit over 40 home runs five different times in his career.

Perhaps the best way to describe Banks was his demeanor. Former managerial great Leo Durocher once commented on the whole "nice guys finish last" thing, saying that Banks was the one nice guy that finished first and had the talent to go with it.

Yogi Berra

Berra played catcher for the New York Yankees and eventually managed both the Yankees and the Mets. Although he was a great player, he could most be remembered for being a "talker." As a catcher he was always trying to disrupt hitters with his antics. In the 1958 World Series he kept trying to tell Hank Aaron to hit the ball with the label on the bat up. Finally, Aaron told him "I'm here to hit, not to read!"

Perhaps the most famous "Yogi-ism" is the cliche we hear so often today. He is credited with being the first one to say "it ain't over til it's over."

Yogi played on fifteen All-Star teams and was on ten World Series winning teams. He was a player who would swing at almost anything, but also possessed the ability to hit almost anything.

In addition to all this, Berra was also a gunners mate on the USS Bayfield that was involved in the D-Day invasion of France.

Nestor Chylak

Inasmuch as the players, their habits, the owners, and the media all effect baseball in a big way, we haven't mentioned the umpires much. So, let's give them their due. Often times we yell at umpires for having what we might think is poor eyesight, but Chylak recovered from a World War II accident that almost left him blind.

His eyes were pelted with shrapnel, and it wasn't just any old war venue, it was the Battle of the Bulge. For that, he was awarded a Bronze Star and a Purple Heart. I wonder if that were to happen in this day and age if we'd give him the same grief. Probably not.

After he recovered and the war was over he began umpiring Minor League games, making his MLB debut in 1954. His career spanned 25 years, and he umpired Sandy Koufax's final game in the 1966 World Series, as well as the Toronto Blue Jays first home game, ever.

For an umpire, he was very well liked by the players, known for his quick wit, and his enthusiasm. Often times umpires would get lax late in a game, wanting it to be over. Not Nestor. He fought the players until the final out.

Joe DiMaggio

It's funny, but true. One of the first things people think about when they think of DiMaggio is that he was a spokesman for Mr. Coffee. What's also true and another off-the-field thing is that he was once married to Marilyn Monroe! So, Joe did alright for himself even aside from his baseball career with the Yankees.

Joe did everything on the field well and seemingly with very little effort. As a result, they nicknamed Joe "The Yankee Clipper," referencing the great sailing ships.

DiMaggio holds many MLB and Yankee records, but the one that stands out to most and the one that many say will never be broken is his 56 game hitting streak.

The Yankees had a centerfielder after Joe, too. Some kid named Mickey Mantle. And if you really want to know how and why the Yankees were so good for so long, all you need to do is look at the beginning of Joe's career. In 1936 he made his debut in the New York lineup, hitting in the batting order in front of another legend, Lou Gehrig.

And as testimony to what a different time and place it was, after the attack on Pearl Harbor his parents, both Italian immigrants, were classified as "enemy aliens."

Sandy Koufax

Sandy has many distinctions, but one that's relevant here is that he was the youngest player inducted into the Hall of Fame in 1971. He only played twelve seasons of professional baseball. His career was shortened by arthritis in his left elbow, so he retired in order to save his arm from a more permanent disability. Koufax pitched for the Dodgers, both in Brooklyn and Los Angeles, and is often referred to as the best-ever left handed pitcher. One year his record was an astonishing 25-5, which prompted yet another "Yogi-ism." Berra said that yes, he could see how Sandy won 25 games, but he could not see how he lost five!

He was the first pitcher to throw four no-hitters, and also the eighth pitcher to throw a perfect game.

When his career was abruptly shortened, Koufax signed a 10-year broadcasting contract with NBC. That deal, in 1967, was for $1 million, which in today's dollars is over $7 million. He quit after six years. On a personal note, Sandy was at one time married to Anne Widmark, daughter of the famous Hollywood icon, Richard Widmark.

And it all almost didn't happen. Sandy was given a basketball scholarship to Cincinnati and had planned on becoming an architect.

Kenesaw Landis

Kenesaw "Mountain" Landis never played the game, at least not professionally. Landis wasn't a manager. He was, however, the first Commissioner of Major League Baseball. Shortly after the Chicago Black Sox scandal we talked about earlier, the two leagues got together to appoint a commissioner.

Landis had been a Federal prosecutor, notably known for taking on big corporations. The leagues wanted someone with a firm hand, at that's exactly what they got. His first order of business was to ban eight White Sox players for having a connection to a New York gambler/gangster. He did this even after the men had been acquitted in court.

He's also part and parcel responsible for the Minor League players having the ability to be called up during the season, as well as introducing the first All-Star game and the first game to be played at night.

He was not just tough on the players. In his first season as Commissioner, the New York Giants owner and manager purchased a race track in Cuba. Remember, this was 1921. After the whole Black Sox thing, he decided that MLB owners simply could not be involved in baseball and horse racing. The owners put the track back on the market.

Landis died in office in 1944, but over those 20-plus years made many important rulings that still effect the game today.

Frank Robinson

Earlier we talked about the Triple Crown, which is the leader of batting average, home runs, and runs batted in, all in the same season. Frank is in an exclusive class of only four players to have won it since Ted Williams did in 1947. That was after Ted came back from the military, and I forgot to mention that Ted won it five years earlier before he left for service, so had there not been WWII, a lot of things would be different, but there might have been little doubt as to who the best hitter ever was.

Robinson broke into MLB at the age of 20, in 1956. He promptly set a rookie record of 38 home runs in a season, and was the Rookie of the Year. He spent the bulk of his career with the Cincinnati Reds, and a handful of very productive years with the Orioles. He toiled with a few other teams over his 20-year playing career.

At the end of his career he became a player/manager for the

Cleveland Indians, and after retiring spent over a decade managing. That includes the now-defunct (or in Washington) Montreal Expos. The stint with Cleveland made him the first African American manager in baseball.

Since there's probably not an award Frank didn't win, nor a big game he never played in or played hard, he's quite deserved of being in Cooperstown on so many levels.

Nolan Ryan

Dale Murphy played most of his career with the Braves, and was a two-time League MVP. He once said that Ryan was the only pitcher you started thinking about two days before you faced him. Ryan began his career with the Mets, but then the military called. Upon his emergence from service and a subsequent trade to the Angels, his career took off. I'm sure the Mets have regrets over that one, since Ryan threw not one, but four no-hitters with the Angels.

In the 1980's Nolan returned home to his native Texas, playing for the Astros, and became the first $1 million player in baseball. He ended up throwing a total of seven no-hitters. Nolan threw 12 one-hitters! He is baseball's all-time strikeout leader with 5714, and to put that into perspective, Randy Johnson is second on that list with 839 less.

He was a dominant and intimidating pitcher, as opposed to those that are simply crafty. Nolan threw the "Ryan's Express" fastball -

and Reggie Jackson once said Ryan was the only pitcher that made him think he needed to wear a batting helmet with an ear flap.

Both on and off the field he's earned everyone's respect for his professionalism. You just don't hear bad things about Nolan, who has also been involved in the front office of several teams since his retirement.

Tom Seaver

This is one pitcher the Mets didn't let get away. Until later. He was voted into the Hall of Fame in 1992 with what was at the time the highest percentage of votes, ever. He pitched for 20 years, and is an elite club with over 300 wins. 311 to be exact. That club has only 24 members, and he pitched back when relief pitchers just didn't really exist. In my opinion, there won't be any new members of that club.

As far as the Mets are concerned, it appears all good things must come to an end. In 1977 Free Agency was started to take hold and Seaver wanted to renegotiate his contract to be paid in line with other top pitchers. The Mets felt Tom's demands were greedy, so on the last day of the trade deadline, shipped him off to Cincinnati for players that are certainly not in our book. That was one of two trades the Mets made that day, and the media and their fans still refer to that day as "The Midnight Massacre," since they also parted ways with Dave Kingman.

Tom was so valuable and revered in New York that he was dubbed

"The Franchise," magnified by the fact that prior to his arrival the Mets had been, well, bad. Almost overnight they were turned into perennial contenders, thanks in no small part to Tom Terrific.

Ozzie Smith

Smith is the real "Wizard of Oz," and not for hitting home runs or stealing bases (although he did do some of that), but for his defensive prowess. If you ask anyone that's alive who the best defensive shortstop ever was, unanimously they will give you Ozzie Smith.

Ozzie won 13 Gold Gloves as the best defensive shortstop, and holds the Major League record for both assists and double plays.

He was also know for running out of the dugout and on to the field doing a patented forward-flip, perhaps as gracefully as Mary Lou Retton.

He started his career with the San Diego Padres and spent four years there. At the time the St. Louis had had about enough of their shortstop, Gary Templeton, and his attitude/antics. Consequently, a trade between the two teams was consummated. There were other players involved, but Smith and Templeton were the centerpieces.

I'll tell you just how clear it was his defense that got him to the Hall of Fame. Over an 18 year career, Smith hit exactly 28 home runs and finished with a .262 career batting average. Those numbers are pedestrian by any standards.

Lou Brock

Brock is another player on a list of players that teams probably regret trading. Lou came into the league with the Chicago Cubs, starting in centerfield in 1962. After only two years the Cubs were desperate for pitching, so they traded Brock to the St. Louis Cardinals for Ernie Broglio. Broglio had won 18 games the previous year, and ended up with exactly 77 for his entire career.

Brock did everything well, but perhaps his biggest asset was on the bases. He had blazing speed and pressured opposing defenses just with his presence on the basepaths.

It didn't take long for Brock to pay the St. Louis dividends. In 1964 he hit .348 with 81 runs scored and 33 stolen bases, leading St. Louis to the NL pennant. He wasn't done yet. He hit .300 in the World Series and led the Cardinals to a win over the New York Yankees.

In 1985 he was elected to the Hall of Fame in just his first year of eligibility, and became just the 20th player at the time to have that happen.

Whitey Ford

We haven't had a Yankee pitcher yet, and now we do. Whitey Ford was the "pitching Ozzie Smith," since he made everything seem effortless. Ford won a higher percentage of his games than any other modern day pitcher. It was a different time and a different era, but Ford was yet another one whose career was interrupted by the military. In 1953, after serving two years in the Army, Ford came back and pitched like he'd never left, going 18-6 and leading the Yankees to yet another World Series title.

Ford holds the record for most post-season consecutive scoreless innings pitched, at 33 1/3, with a 2.71 ERA. Many pitchers can do good things it when it matters less, Ford did it when it mattered most, in the clutch.

When Yogi Berra passed away in 2015, accomplished New York writer George Vecsey then referred to Ford as the "now the greatest living Yankee legend."

I think most pitchers doctored a baseball at one time or another, and Ford admitted to doing it in an All-Star game, striking out Willie Mays.

Tommy Lasorda

We haven't had many managers make our book, and no managerial list would be complete without Tommy Lasorda. There may have been managers with better records and/or longevity, but few were as colorful as Lasorda.

Lasorda was the face of the Dodgers for almost three decades. He won 1599 games, and even after his managing days were over, he stayed in baseball. He came out of retirement to manage the US baseball team in the 2000 Olympics. He coached third base in the 2001 All-Star game, but even after all the accomplishments, that might not have been what most remember him for.

Tommy was famous for his colorful tirades, both on and off the field. Some of his obscenity-laced rants about players, managers, the front office, and umpires are the stuff of underground legends, if you can find them. If nothing else, you knew where you stood with Lasorda.

Jim Rice

Jim was the third left fielder in almost five decades for the Boston Red Sox. He was preceded by Carl Yaztrzemski, who was preceded by Ted Williams, who are all in the Hall of Fame. I told you there was something special about playing in front of that Green Monster for many years.

Rice also played his entire career in Boston, at a time when free agency was a big deal. During his 12 year career, Jim hit 352 home runs, only surpassed in that span by Dave Kingman and Mike Schmidt.

Jim was very active as a philanthropist. He was named the Honorary Chairman of the Jimmy Fund, which for those that aren't familiar with Boston, is the primary fund raising agent for the Dana Farber Cancer Institute.

Rice was not elected to the Hall of Fame until his 15th and final year of eligibility, for which there is much speculation as to why. Perhaps the most likely reason was his relationship with the media, which was never harmonious. Unfortunately, many of those same media people are members of the Baseball Writers Association of America, who of course are the core Hall of Fame voters.

Bud Selig

Let's look at a contemporary Commissioner. Bud Selig was the Commissioner from 1998 until 2015, so unfortunately for him that encompassed most of the "steroid" era. He was perhaps tougher on some things than he should have been, and not rigid enough on others, most notably the steroids. He's quite candid about it since leaving office, or more accurately was forced out by a 19-8 "no confidence" vote by the owners.

One could ask why he's in the Hall of Fame. The fact was that in spite of the clouds, he did a lot of very progressive things in his tenure.

There were Division realignment and the addition of Wild Card teams to the playoffs, and the addition of Interleague play. Of course he implemented many new drug testing policies, which on the surface one might think he could just "do," and it was all done over almost a decade or legal wrangling with the owners, who he works for, and the Players Union, so you can imagine why it took a entire decade.

He added instant replay.

For a time, he was even an adjunct teacher at Marquette Law School, lecturing on collective bargaining, anti-trust, revenue sharing, and even the intellectual property rights. And trust me, nobody was more qualified to do that. So, although some might view Bud as a stain on the game, he was thrust into a job in a time and a place that conditions were very difficult. To have come out the other side of that with his integrity and have accomplished all that he did in spite of the obstacles, he ought to have his own Hall of Fame!

RANDOM FUN FACTS

1. Before being named Commissioner of baseball, Bud Selig was part owner of the Milwaukee Brewers.

2. Abner Doubleday was a Major General in the US Army and is buried at Arlington National Cemetery.

3. A mint condition Nolan Ryan Rookie card is valued at $35,000.

4. An authenticated autographed Jackie Robinson baseball is listed on eBay for $9,900. I actually thought it would be more than that.

5. If you've got a spare $20,000 you can buy yourself a game-used, autographed Joe DiMaggio jersey, tax included.

6. A ball signed by Babe Ruth, on the open market, is worth about $80,000.

7. Pete Rose signed a baseball with the words "I'm sorry I bet on baseball." It's only $149. If Pete didn't bet on baseball and were in the Hall of Fame, it'd be worth 50 times that.

8. A lot of players won't sign memorabilia, knowing that many times their signatures are on eBay within hours, and not in some kids' bedroom as a treasure.

9. The fact that many players won't sign is why there are

memorabilia shows around the country are so popular. The players get paid to sign. They don't need the money, they're just not going to be bastardized.

10. Quinn Wolcott was the youngest MLB umpire ever when he made his debut in 2013 at the age of 30.

11. Bruce Froemming was the oldest umpire in MLB but the real oddity was that he was on the field for 11 no-hitters.

12. During the regular season there is an umpire at every base. In the post-season they add one down each outfield line, for a total of six.

13. Steve Carlton, most of his career spent with the Phillies, holds the MLB record for the most balks. He had 90 during his career.

14. Pitching for the Milwaukee Braves in 1963, Bob Shaw had five balks in one game.

15. Ricky Guittierez, playing for the Houston Astros at the time, holds the record for the most pitches seen in one at-bat. Twenty.

16. The 1908 St. Louis Cardinals were shut out 33 times. By contrast, five teams have gone an entire season without ever being shut out.

17. Daniel Nava, at the time with the Boston Red Sox, hit a home run in his first-ever at-bat in MLB. It was a Grand Slam, and it

was on the first pitch he saw.

18. There have been 22 players to homer in their first MLB at-bat that never hit another one.

19. Cy Young holds two records that will probably never be broken. He has 511 career wins, and pitched 749 complete games. The next closest on the win list, Walter Johnson, has 94 less wins.

20. In 1999 Fernando Tatis hit two Grand Slams in one game. That's been done several times, but Tatis did it in one inning.

TEST YOURSELF – QUESTIONS AND ANSWERS

1. Who holds the record for most consecutive games with a hit, at 56?

   A. Ty Cobb
   B. Pete Rose
   C. Joe DiMaggio

2. The career record for strikeouts by a pitcher is held by whom?

   A. Cy Young
   B. Sandy Koufax
   C. Nolan Ryan

3. What HOF pitcher holds the record for the most consecutive scoreless post-season innings?

   A. Tom Seaver
   B. Nolan Ryan
   C. Whitey Ford

4. Who succeeded Ted Williams and Carl Yastrzemski as the left-fielder for the Boston Red Sox?

   A. Frank Robinson
   B. Jim Rice

C.   Lou Brock

5.   What MLB Commissioner banned eight White Sox players from the Hall of Fame?

   A.   Bud Selig
   B.   Kenesaw Landis
   C.   Nestor Chylak

ANSWERS

1. C
2. C
3. C
4. B
5. B

CHAPTER SIX:

DEFINING MOMENTS

We've talked at length about the people, places, and things that make up baseball. The list could go on forever, but whether the players, managers, or umpires were famous or not, many were involved in what were once-in-a-lifetime moments.

You know the type. The events that you remember where you were when they happened. I'll share one of my personal ones that you might be able to relate to.

My Dad took me to many Red Sox games as a kid, and one in particular was a game against the Baltimore Orioles, if memory serves me right. It was perhaps the 6th inning or so when there was a big hush in the crowd.

As a young lad I really wondered what the heck I was missing. It was July 20th, 1969, and I was all of twelve years old. What was going on? Nothing was happening on the field. It was the moment Neil Armstrong and Buzz Aldrin landed on the moon.

Let's look at some moments that for at least a minute or two, polarized the baseball world.

SHORTEST HOME RUN

Andy Oyler had a Major League career that spanned exactly 29 games for the Baltimore Orioles in 1902. Now, of course not many readers will remember what Andy did, or have ever heard of Andy. In his brief career, he hit exactly one home run in 77 at bats. But, that home run goes down as the shorted one ever hit, and in fact never left the infield. Rumor has it that the ball traveled about six feet.

The story goes that in the bottom of the ninth inning, Oyler ducked while at the plate to avoid a pitch coming in at his head. The ball hit the bat and stuck in the mud only a few inches in front of home plate.

Oyler was able to run the bases and complete an inside-the-park home run before anyone could find the ball.

THE BRAWL - 1993

The Seattle Mariners were playing the Baltimore Orioles, and there were multiple brawls, not just one bench-clearing incident. Mariners' Bill Haselman had hit a home run earlier in the game, and is often the case in their next at bat the pitcher would throw what's known as a "purpose pitch," or brush him back to make a point.

Mike Mussina promptly drilled Haselman in the back. The benches emptied.

In what ensued, Chris Bosio of the Mariners broke his collarbone. Oddly, he had just come back from the disabled list - for a broken collarbone. Eventually the Baltimore police came on the field, but not to break up the fights. They had to keep the fans off the field! The real irony here, aside from being one of the biggest brawls in history, is that Cal Ripken thought he'd have to sit out the next day with a sore knee. He did not, and the rest, as they say, is history.

HANK AARON'S RECORD BREAKER

This one I remember as if it were yesterday. Most of us know that Babe Ruth hit 714 home runs in his career, and most of us know the first person to break that record, Hank Aaron, did so in 1974.

He had a chance to break it in the final game of the previous season, but didn't. Because Aaron is an African American, over the course of that winter he received numerous death threats! His only comment was that he might not live to see 1974. But, he did.

He actually got a plaque from the US Postal Service for receiving more mail than anyone, other than a politician.

What's interesting here is that the Braves played the first three games of that season in Cincinnati, and of course Braves fans and executives wanted the record broken in Atlanta. He had planned on sitting out the series, but the Commissioner ruled he had to play in two of the games. In his very first at bat he homered to tie the record, but didn't hit another one in the series. Maybe on purpose, who knows.

Then, on April 8th, with a crowd of over 53,000 on hand, in the bottom of the fourth inning, he deposited an Al Downing pitch into the stands for number 715. Even though baseball was more or less in its television infancy, it seemed like the world was watching.

Even more ironic is that legendary basketball broadcaster Craig Sager, then a very young man, interviewed Aaron between third base and home plate. Basketball fans may know that Sager recently lost a battle to cancer.

MCGUIRE & SOSA CHASE MARIS

In the late summer and early fall of 1988 there was a race to break Roger Maris' record of 61 home runs in a season. Several players had come close over the years, but none had broken the record. This year, it was clear that either Mark McGuire or Sammy Sosa, or both, were going to get hit more than 61 home runs. It wasn't if, it was when.

It was back and forth all summer, each would hit a few, then the other would catch up. The two acting like best of friends both on and off the field, playing to the crowds. Sammy Sosa with his patented "V" sign after every dinger, dedicated to the late Cubs broadcaster Harry Caray.

It was almost as if the two had scripted the moments along the way. Then came September 7th when McGuire's Cardinals were to play a two-game series against Sosa's Cubs, as fate would have it. Again, seemingly scripted. In the first game, McGuire sat a 60, and hit one over the fence to tie Maris. The very next night he hit number 62, the record breaker, off of Steve Trachsel.

The two went back and forth the final month, almost seemingly letting the other one catch up to create more drama. McGuire finished with 70 that season, shattering Maris' record, while Sosa finished with 66.

And of course, that was the beginning of the steroid controversy. McGuire was never "proven" to have taken them, but upon retirement he did admit to using them in an interview with Bob Costas.

1994 STRIKE

It was actually called a "work stoppage," to be fair. It was perhaps the darkest moment in baseball for many true fans of the game, and still is for those of us who remember.

This was not the first work stoppage, but it was the most costly to the game, which is one reason why perhaps baseball looked the other way during the McGuire/Bonds chase and several other "super-human" performances as they relate to steroids, because it brought fans back.

The strike started in August, and they never resumed play that year, and it's still the only time in the modern era that we didn't have a World Series. It even had an effect on Michael Jordan, the basketball great, since he signed a contract to play baseball for the White Sox. Baseball needed players, and here was Jordan's chance.

With still no compromise in the spring of 1995 and Spring Training about to start, the league discussed using replacement players as the NFL had done years earlier. Multi-million dollar television deals collapsed. Then, on March 28th, a US District Court judge upheld the NLRB's earlier ruling that there had indeed been unfair labor practices by the owners. And yet the owners voted 27-3 to start the season with replacement players.

Attendance that year dropped 20%. Perhaps the biggest impact was felt by the Montreal Expos, and as we mentioned earlier, they were forced to sell their high-priced players and eventually leave town for Washington. It's considered the most costly "work-stoppage" in US history.

TOMMY JOHN SURGERY

Tommy John was a pitcher for the Dodgers, but most may know him for "Tommy John" surgery. In 1974 he came out of a game against the Montreal Expos with pain in his throwing elbow, the left one. It was diagnosed as a tear in his ulnar collateral ligament, and of course 40-plus years ago most figured his career was simply over.

Instead, he had a radical surgery that involved replacing the ligament with a tendon from his right forearm. Most thought he'd lead a normal life and fade away into the sunset. However, he rehabbed and pitched effectively in 1976. So, not only did he come back to pitch, he pitched until he was 46 years old. He ended up winning 288 games, and now "Tommy John" surgery is pretty common, with over a 90% success rate.

The downside, however, is that now even 12-year-old kids are throwing curveballs, and a great many twenty-something pitchers are coming in almost as damaged goods. Honestly, sometimes I think the mindset anymore is that they'll just have the same surgery Tommy John did and be fine. So, Tommy John was a great player, but remembered more for the successful and radical surgery.

ROSE PASSES TY COBB

We all, or at least most do, know that Pete Rose is the all-time hit leader. In August of 1981 he passed Stan Musial on the list, who had been second behind Cobb. Stan was actually in the crowd to congratulate Pete. Then in September (the 11th to be exact) he passed Ty Cobb for the all-time lead. Marge Schott, then the owner of the Cincinnati Reds, gave Pete a red corvette with the license plate PR-4192, obviously in reference to the hit number that broke the record.

At the time, Pete Rose was one of baseball's most beloved players, and even more so on that night because Cobb was one of the most reviled. So, as Jayson Stark of ESPN said later, "it was all so clear, until it wasn't."

Pete had gambled on baseball, and on his own team, while playing and managing. But, that night belonged to Pete, and now of course he is banned from the game. Ever the capitalist, today he lives in Las Vegas, because of course gambling is legal in Nevada. He earns over $1 million a year signing autographs and through public appearances. In fact, he has an annual appearance in Cooperstown around the time of the Hall of Fame induction ceremonies, but cannot stay with the other players at the Oswego resort nor can he attend the ceremonies!

He has even appeared in WWE wrestling events! In his autobiography, "My Prison Without Bars," he finally came clean with it all. Pete's never been boring, but for over two decades he gave baseball many of its most memorable moments.

CLEMENTE KILLED IN A PLANE CRASH

Earlier we touched on Roberto Clemente's accomplishments both on and off the field. But, the day his plane went down parallels the Buddy Holly crash in terms of public captivation. When Buddy died, Don MacLean wrote a song called "American Pie," and the lyrics reflect that tragedy as the "day the music died." When Clemente's plane crashed, that had the same effect on baseball - complete shock.

There hasn't been anyone to my knowledge that has said a bad word about Roberto off the field, or on it. That day in 1972 marks one of the most tragic days the sport has or ever will see. What made it and Roberto even bigger than life itself is that he was also a national hero in Puerto Rico.

In the midst of a humanitarian relief effort for earthquake victims in Nicaragua, Clemente's plane took off over two tons overweight and crashed into the Atlantic Ocean a mere two minutes after takeoff. His body was never found.

People refer to December 7th, 1941, as the "day that will live in infamy" for the attack on Pearl Harbor, and New Years' Eve of 1972 has that same correlation with Major League Baseball.

PSA, a well-known memorabilia authenticator, grades baseball cards on a scale of 1-10. They've graded roughly 375,000 of Roberto's Rookie Card as a"9," or mint condition. They're worth upwards of $400,000 each. They've graded exactly ONE as "Gem Mint," or a "10." I can only imagine what it might be worth on the open market. For sure, that was one card I ruined in my bicycle spokes.

SPORTS ILLUSTRATED STORY ON STERIODS

The year was 2002 and that was several years after the McGuire/Sosa home run race, and by then the rumors were rampant, but nobody was talking. Players knew. Managers knew. But it wasn't until Sports Illustrated published "The Story," that everyone became fully aware of what was going on. A lot of people like to think that the Mitchell Report, and independent study commissioned by baseball and published in 2007, was the deal-breaker. It really wasn't.

There are those that will point to Jose Canseco's book, "Juiced," as the tell-all. Jose did use steroids and will do or say just about anything for attention, but it was Sports Illustrated who published an article years earlier that is regarded as the actual "Pandora's Box."

In the article, Ken Caminiti, who played most of his career with the Houston Astros, spoke at length about using steroids to recover from an injury. He found out how much they increased his production, and just kept using them. The article also had stories from Kenny Rogers and Curt Shilling (yes, the "bloody sock" guy) who wouldn't name names, but made some vivid claims. Knowing today how outspoken Schilling is, I'm sure it was all true.

The SI article was three years before Canseco's book and a full five years before the Mitchell Report. The only real difference from the article to the Mitchell Report was that the latter named names.

Canseco estimated that at the time that 85% of Major League Baseball players were using performance enhancing drugs.

THE MAD DASH

People use that term in many different ways. The dictionary refers to a "mad dash" as a wild and uncontrolled rush," and in 1946 that's what people refer to Enos Slaugher's run to home plate in the seventh game of the 1946 World Series as - The "Mad Dash."

It's said that it was another of the key moments that kept the Curse of the Bambino alive, which is known as the sale of Babe Ruth to New York that kept haunting Boston.

The game was tied. Remember, it's the decisive seventh game, and it was the 8th inning. That's about as tight as a game and a series can get. Enos singled to start the inning, and two batters later, with two outs, there he was still at first base.

The Cardinals called for a "hit and run," which was executed perfectly. Slaughter took off, and although the ball didn't roll all the way to the wall, that didn't slow Slaughter down. He just kept running, and Boston's shortstop, Johnny Pesky, was so surprised Slaughter kept running that he threw late to home plate. Enos scored what was the winning run, extending Boston's misery one more year.

BUCKY DENT'S HOME RUN

As a Boston Red Sox fan, this is a moment in time that I can tell you exactly where I was and what I was doing. The year was 1978 and it was one of the most devastating blows to Boston, perhaps even more so than the Bill Buckner error.

It was magnified by the fact that it was against the Yankees. The two teams had tied for the American League East, and had to play a one-game tie breaker. I don't remember why, but it was "advantage Boston," because the game was played at Fenway Park. It was a weekday, and it was a workday. But, most of New England stopped whatever they were doing, including work, at lunchtime.

Boston had already blown a huge lead in the regular season, while

New York finished 39-14 to force the playoff.

The Red Sox took a 2-0 lead into the 7th inning. There was hope after all.

But wait, this was the Yankees.

They had two men on base and there were two outs, with the ninth hitter in the lineup due up. Bucky Dent.

Of course he promptly hit a home run, that was basically nothing more than a routine fly ball in most parks, but it was in the direction of the Green Monster. The wall tall enough to turn would-be home runs into singles, or in this case, it turned an almost routine into a three run home run.

Dent played 12 seasons of Major League Baseball and hit a total of 40 home runs. Never more than five in one year. But if he only hit one, that was the one that mattered and the one everyone knows him for, and where they were at the time.

THE BABE CALLS HIS SHOT

Many people may have heard of it, and as kids many of us tried to emulate it. Babe Ruth calling a home run. Pointing out to centerfield before he hit it, is the subject of both lore and controversy.

Since there wasn't an ESPN in 1932, there's no way to know what exactly happened, but it's more fun to think it happened just like the legend has it. Although, whatever the gesture was, it is on film.

What most do agree on is that Ruth said or did something before he belted one over the fence.

It was in a game against the Cubs, and apparently the Cubs and their fans were heckling Ruth to no end. With two strikes, the verbal abuse escalated in anticipation of a strikeout.

Henry Root, the Cubs pitcher at the time, said there was never a "called shot," but what would we expect him to say? The Cubs catcher also disputes the claim, but by the same token his comment was, "I don't want to take anything from the Babe, he's the reason we all made good money."

If only today's players had that kind of self-control with their mouths.

FDR AND THE GREEN LIGHT LETTER

The year was 1942 and of course that was right smack in the middle of World War II. It's impossible for those that weren't alive to understand how baseball had become so important in everyday lives. But, you can imagine that it was at least a diversion from reality for most, not unlike like sports are in today. Sports are still just a game, but also a diversion from the stress of daily life and a rallying point for fans of like kind.

The Commissioner at the time was still Kenesaw Landis, who apparently wasn't sure how to move forward with baseball. Aside from the obvious, baseball had lost many of its stars to the military, making it even harder to imagine the position Landis must have been in.

In an effort to reach clarity, Landis eventually reached out to President Roosevelt. FDR responded as many would have, writing a letter back to Landis that apparently stressed the need for the recreation and distraction.

That letter became known as "The Green Light" letter, since it in effect gave baseball and Landis the green light to play ball.

2001 - BASEBALL RETURNS

After the horrors of 9/11, nobody knew how to react or what to do. The questions abounded as to whether to continue to live normally, stop doing anything, or somewhere in between. Finding a sense of normalcy became paramount.

During September, baseball is in its stretch run, also known as the pennant race. Understandably, baseball and basically everything else in the US was just shut down. The question became, for everyone, what to do next.

Ten days later baseball would resume, and fittingly in New York. The Mets played the Braves in what was the first major sporting event after the attack.

After a huge ceremony, the teams met on the field in a show of solidarity, which was magnified even more by the fact that these two had been division foes and not really the best of friends for years. It signaled "normalcy" of sorts.

That night was much more than a baseball game.

Mike Piazza, the Mets catcher, hit a two-run home run late in the game to put the Mets, the eventual winners, ahead. But, it was more than a game, a hit, and a win. It provided a sense that everything was going to be OK.

BONDS BREAKS AARON'S HOME RUN RECORD

Nobody seemed to care, and in fact, it turned into a fiasco for many. In 2007 he hit home run number 756 to pass Babe Ruth as baseball's all-time home run leader. It should have been epic, and to some degree it was. For all the wrong reasons.

By this time it was fairly evident, although not proven, that Bonds' production was most likely due to his use of steroids. He had been heckled and booed in almost every road park he played in that year.

So, although much of that is fairly well-known, what's not is common knowledge is that both Hank Aaron and the Commissioner, Bud Selig, were not at the game. Aaron did show his graciousness, recording a message to be played on the scoreboard when the record broken.

We know Bonds remains out of the Hall of Fame. Had that home run been hit by someone the public didn't really like, they'd have stopped the game for an hour. As it were, it was merely an afterthought outside the City of San Francisco.

FATHER AND SON

Ken Griffey Sr, played Major League Baseball for 18 years and for a handful of different teams. He's perhaps most know as being part of the Cincinnati Reds during their dominant years in the mid-1970. He was a well above-average player and hit almost .300 for his career.

His son, Ken Griffey, Jr, who most of today's generation knows far more about, is already in baseball's Hall of Fame. But, there was a very special moment in August of 1990. They became the first father and son to play on the same team. But wait, it gets better.

On September 14th of that year, they hit back-to-back home runs. That had obviously never been done before, and his highly unlikely to happen again.

EBBETS FIELD DEMOLISHED

Ebbets Field opened in 1913, and was set in the Flatbush section of Brooklyn. It was the home of the Brooklyn Dodgers, but was also the home to not one, but three National Football League teams in its lifetime.

Ebbets Field saw more than its fair share of classic moments, one of which was actually a "double header" of sorts. The year was 1938 and the park was holding its first-ever night game. That in and of itself would be a moment, but it's also the game that

Johnny Vander Meer threw his second consecutive no-hitter.

Ebbets Field was also the site of Jackie Robinson's first game.

The story of the Dodgers and their move to Los Angeles has been chronicled by numerous books, and was also worked into the famous Kevin Costner movie, "Field of Dreams."

In 1960 Ebbets Field was auctioned off and demolished, and now is the site of apartment buildings, which were renamed Jackie Robinson Apartments in 1972, the year he passed away.

RANDOM FUN FACTS

1. Ted Williams once reached base in sixteen consecutive plate appearances.

2. Williams won not one, but two Triple Crowns. He came so close to winning a third, which would have been truly epic, but in 1949 he lost the batting title by .0016.

3. In 1983, Orioles pitcher Tippy Martinez did something that not only had never been done, but it's a record that can never be broken. He picked three base runners off in one inning.

4. With seven no-hitters it's no surprise that Nolan Ryan threw them in three different decades. Pitcher Hideo Nomo had two no-hitters, in two different centuries.

5. We know the Atlanta Braves franchise originated in Boston, but we didn't know that for one year they were called the Beaneaters, after Boston baked beans.

6. Baseball stopped being an Olympic sport after a vote by International Olympic Committee in 2012.

7. Richie Ashburn of the Phillies once fouled off two consecutive pitches, far from uncommon. But what is uncommon is that both of them hit the same woman.

8. The youngest player in history was Joe Nuxhall, who was just

15 when he pitched for the first time.

9. All baseballs are created equal. They've got to have exactly 118 stitches.

10. Catchers wear plenty of padding and protection. Their equipment is often called "The Tools of Ignorance" because no smart people would play that position.

11. As it turns out, catchers are some of the most successful managers in history, so #10 just isn't true.

12. In 1930, Babe Ruth's salary was $80,000. In 2017 dollars that equates to $1.15 million.

13. Babe was asked that year why he deserved to make more than the US President, Hebert Hoover. His response was "because I had a better year."

14. There are more than 100 Countries in the International Baseball Federation, so I guess it's not just America's favorite pastime anymore.

15. The first baseball game to be aired on television was between the Cincinnati Reds and the Brooklyn Dodgers in 1939.

16. Baseball, motherhood, apple pie, and of course, hot dogs. In 2014 over 21 million of them were served at ballparks.

17. Reggie Jackson is the only player to win a home run title with three different teams.

18. Kaz Matsui is just another in a long list of Japanese players.

But, he's the only one to hit a home run in his first at bat of the season in three consecutive years.

19. We know Jackie Robinson has his number retired by every team. What we didn't know is that Nolan Ryan is the only player to have his number retired by three different teams.

20. Atlanta Braves pitcher Jorge Sosa had exactly three hits in 2006. All three of them left the park.

TEST YOURSELF – QUESTIONS AND ANSWERS

1. In 1998 which two players both passed Roger Maris for most home runs in a season?

   A. Barry Bonds and Pete Rose

   B. Mark McGuire and Sammy Sosa

   C. Ken Griffey and Roberto Clemente

2. What pitcher had a ligament replaced in his elbow and now has a surgical procedure named after him?

   A. Tom Seaver

   B. Whitey Ford

   C. Tommy John

3. What famous St. Louis Cardinal player made "The Mad Dash" to keep Boston from winning a title?

   A. Enos Slaughter

   B. Ken Griffey, Sr.

   C. Pete Rose

4. Who did Pete Rose pass in 1981 for the most career hits?

   A. Ty Cobb

   B. Babe Ruth

   C. Ted Williams

5. What US President wrote "The Green Light Letter" to the then Commissioner Kenesaw Landis?

   A. Herbert Hoover
   B. Franklin Roosevelt
   C. Calvin Coolidge

ANSWERS

1. B
2. C
3. A
4. A
5. B

CHAPTER SEVEN:
THE BEST OF THE REST

We've covered a lot, and we could spend another ten chapters covering what would be considered heroic, relevant, or just plain strange. But, all good things must come to an end. In this chapter we'll look at some of the lesser-known events and people, many of which may be pertinent and relevant to certain teams, or certain parts of the country, but no less a big part of baseball history. If I've left anyone out or anything off, it's certainly not been my intent.

SEATTLE PILOTS

The Seattle Pilots may be baseball's shining example of how to go from beginning to end in a relatively short period of time. We know they were from Seattle, and one might think they were named the Pilots as a reference to Boeing, which is in part, true. But the original owner was a part-time harbor pilot! They had egos, then, too.

They were established as an expansion team in 1969, and their on-field play was the least of their problems. They initially played in Sicks Stadium, which was at the time a state-of-the-art Minor

League stadium. As part of the original agreement with MLB to get a franchise, the stadium was supposed to be expanded to hold 30,000 fans. But by Opening Day, it only held 19,500 and it was all downhill from there.

The long story short, in 1970, one year later, they filed for bankruptcy and moved to Milwaukee.

AT & T Park

The home of the San Francisco Giants since 2000, it was formerly known as Pac Bell Park. I guess AT & T had a bigger checkbook. Actually, that's not true. Pacific Bell bought the naming rights for $50 million in 1996 over a 24 year period. Pac-Bell had been purchased by SBC Communications, and the stadium took that name for a period of time.

Then of course SBC bought AT & T, and here we are today. That's the rule rather than the exception with naming rights, though, as it's all about the money.

What's perhaps the most interesting and unique feature of the park is that home runs to right field that are long enough sail out of the park and into San Francisco Bay. That particular body of water is now named McCovey Cove, after long-time Giant great, Willie McCovey.

It's standard operating procedure to see any number of kayaks floating around during a game, hoping to catch more than a fish. In bigger games such as World Series game, it's a flotilla.

WRIGLEY FIELD

Of course we need to talk about one of the oldest parks and one that's still in use today. Its ivy covered outfield walls are simply legendary. But what I'd like to share is once again, is the value of the dollar.

The stadium broke ground in 1911 and was first opened in 1914. The total cost of construction is reported to have been $250,000.

Today, there are PSL's (Personal Seat Licenses) that sell for that much.

In 1912, the average salary for a steelworker was $630. Today, it's over $56,000 and perhaps part of the reason the industry is all but gone in the United States.

In 1908 the cost of a Hershey bar was two cents, so yes, we've evolved. Or have we?

HARVEY HADDIX

Pitching a no-hitter or a perfect game has been done many times, and we've talked about some of the epic ones. But throwing a no-hitter or a perfect game and losing is a pretty rare occurrence. But, Harvey Haddix did it.

In 1953 he threw not only a no-hitter, but a perfect game, for twelve innings. The perfect game was ended by a fielding error. Haddix then walked the next batter, and in what was at the time controversial, Joe Adcock hit a home run and the Cardinals lost the game. Braves' pitcher Lew Burdette was throwing a shutout!

On the bright side, Haddix was the winning pitcher when Bill Mazeroski hit his famous home run in the 1960 World Series.

There have been times where someone threw a no-hitter and lost, but never a perfect game.

THE EVOLUTION OF THE BALL

In the good old days, you know, the 1800's, the ball varied in both size and weight. They were made from a rubber core, and wrapped with yarn and leather. In the 1850's baseball at least tried to regulate the weight and circumference, but there were still some pretty big variations, as balls were between 5.5-6 ounces. Remember, of course, that they were all handmade, so there's no chance of uniformity like we have with automation.

In 1934 the AL and NL came to a compromise and decided to try standardize things a bit more. If nothing else, all the balls had to have a cork center and a horsehide cover.

In 1974, balls were switched from horsehide to cowhide. Of course there were numerous tweaks in the interim, but those were some of the bigger changes.

Then came the juiced ball era. Although it's never been proven, it's suggested that the balls were altered in the 1990's in an effort to increase scoring. This theory came back to forefront in 2016 with the fact that the number of home runs dramatically increased. It is more than likely that it's a combination of juiced balls and steroids, because there are still players to this day that are getting caught cheating.

THE EVOLUTION OF THE GLOVE

The first baseball games were actually played bare-handed, and in fact when they did first use "gloves," they were merely a tool to stop the ball from rolling so they could pick it up, rather than as a catching aide.

It is said that the first player to wear a glove was Doug Allison in 1870, but apparently that was more because of an injured hand than a glove to catch the ball. The first confirmed glove was used by Charlie Watt (not the Rolling Stones' drummer, that's Watts), a Cardinal outfielder.

Fast forward to today and Rawlings, the largest baseball glove manufacturer, claims that about half of the players use custom gloves varying in price from the $39.99 ones you can get at Target, all the way into the $1000's for personal MLB gloves.

There are even different types of leather. There's full-grain, kip leather, cowhide, and even premium steer hide. And you thought farmers raised cows only for us to eat at the ball park.

GLOBAL BASEBALL

We know that baseball was played professionally in Canada, first by the Montreal Expos and now by the Toronto Blue Jays. But, the first Major League game played outside of the US or Canada wasn't played until 1996.

It was a three-game series between the Padres and the Mets, played in Monterrey, Mexico. Quite likely it was also an attempt to increase the San Diego fan base, since San Diego isn't that far from Mexico.

In 2000, Major League Baseball opened its season in Japan. They've done that every four years since. Then, in 2014, the Los Angeles Dodgers and the Arizona Diamondbacks played a two-game series in Australia, at the Sydney Cricket Grounds. In fact, as of this writing there are six Australian-born players in Major League Baseball. Interestingly enough, four of them are pitchers, and two of them debuted in 2016.

THE DESIGNATED HITTER

To this day, the pitcher in the National League takes a regular spot in the batting order. Typically, and more so now in the age of specialization, pitchers are just not very good hitters because it's just not something they practice. However, the same cannot be said for the American League.

Pitchers don't bat in the AL. There's a spot in the lineup for a "designated hitter," who does not play in the field. That change was put into place in 1973.

In April of that year, Ron Bloomberg took the first at-bat as a designated hitter against Luis Tiant, and he walked. That year the

American League had a higher batting average than the National League, and it has been the same story every year since.

The DH, as it's known, wasn't immediately adopted in the World Series, but it finally was in 1986. Now, when the American League is the home team both teams use the DH, and neither team does in the National League Park.

Without a doubt whether you have a DH or you don't, both require an entirely different managerial strategy, before and during a game.

ALL IN THE FAMILY

We talked not long ago about the father-and-son duo, the Griffey's. We talked about their amazing feat of playing on the same team and hitting consecutive home runs. There have been other notable all-in-the-family moments as well, which include sibling rivalries.

Gaylord and Jim Perry, both had lengthy and productive careers from the early 1960's to the mid-1970's. Jim won over 200 games in his career, and Gaylord is a member of the elite group of pitchers that won 300! In 1973, they pitched against each other for opposing teams, obviously, but it wasn't the first team it had ever happened.

Back in the 1920's, Jesse and Virgil Barnes threw against each other five times, while Joe and Phil Niekro pitched against each other nine times in the 60's and 70's.

There have been four other lesser-known pitchers/incidents of that happening, the most recent being Jared and Jeff Weaver. Jared is still quite playing for the San Diego Padres. Perhaps the least known but highest profile pitcher to do it was Pedro Martinez, another Hall of Fame player who could easily have had a place in this book. In 1996 while with the Expos, he faced his brother Ramon, who was hurling for the Cubs. It was a rare loss for Pedro, and in fact most of the match ups have been won by the "lesser known" pitcher. I hesitate to call them the "worse" pitcher, because based on the odds of playing professional baseball they've got to be pretty darned good.

SOUR GRAPES

The year was 1904 and the incident is possibly the dictionary definition of sour grapes, and even possibly arrogance. John Brush was President of the National League champion New York Giants, and refused to play the American League champion Boston Americans, aka the Red Sox, in the World Series.

Hence, the 1904 World Series was canceled.

At the time the American League was in its infancy and many National League owners considered the AL inferior, even though Boston was the defending champion. One could point to 1904 as what might have been the beginning of today's rivalry between the Yankees and Boston.

Due to the public fallout and terrible damage it did to his personal reputation, he had a change of heart. His new stance led to a series of "Brush Rules," a set of rules governing on-field play and off-field financing, most of which are still used today.

Perhaps the biggest personal loss that year was that Cy Young would never pitch in a World Series again.

GO WEST YOUNG MAN

Since you've read most of this book, if you stop and think you might recall that most of the defining moments and players with large legacies all came in Boston, New York, Cleveland, and some other East Coast cities. There's a real good reason for that.

Major League Baseball wasn't played West of St. Louis until the year 1955, and one might assume it was in California. But, it wasn't.

It was a game played in Kansas City between the Kansas City A's and the Detroit Tigers.

The A's were a mediocre team, but one of their claims to fame was having an eccentric owner, Arnie Johnson. He was a former associate of Yankee General Manager Dan Topping, and constantly trading away his best players - to the Yankees.

Among those traded away were Clete Boyer and Ralph Terry, two very successful players, and then a guy named Roger Maris.

LET'S PLAY THREE

These days double-headers are rarely actually scheduled, and usually only played as a result of a previous rainout. But, there was a time when they were quite frequently on the schedule. Ernie Banks of the Cubs was famous for saying "let's play two," but I don't think he ever said "let's play three."

But, there was indeed once a triple header.

In 1920 the Reds and the Pirates played what was the first, and last, triple header. Now, "playing three" is prohibited by baseball's CBA, or Collective Bargaining Agreement.

As I understand it, there may have been some triple headers played back in the early 1800's, but baseball has had a different set of rules since 1903 and many of the statistics prior to that year just aren't factored into the record books.

INDOOR HOME RUN

We've talked about a lot of "firsts" in baseball, and there are so many we've missed that we could write another book. We talked about the first game played under a roof, which was obviously in the first domed stadium, the Houston Astrodome.

It wasn't "official," because it was an exhibition game between the New York Yankees and the Houston Astros. There had to be a first walk, first hit, first run, and a first home run. The latter is always the one people will remember, and often times these "firsts" are accomplished by a little-known player. Not this one.

The first home run hit indoors was hit by none other than Mickey Mantle himself.

That stadium had another interesting first as well. In 1973 the Phillies' Mike Schmidt, known for his power, hit a ball that smacked into a speaker hanging from the roof. According to the ground rules, and although the ball would have left the park, the ball is in play. Schmidt made it to first base.

They still have that issue at Tropicana Field in Tampa Bay today.

BEATING EVERONE

Al Leiter was a Major League pitcher for eighteen years and six different teams. Today, he's one of the better broadcasters, making his living calling baseball games for the MLB Network. He's done so many things in his life that I'm green with envy, and now he's talking about running for political office in his home state of New Jersey.

As you might imagine, he won the Roberto Clemente Award, and was a two-time All Star. So, he's got many "claims to fame" for sure.

Al was the first pitcher, ever, to notch a win against all thirty Major League teams. That would also mean you'd have to beat at least one of your former teams.

Rick Wise, as we mentioned earlier, threw a no-hitter and hit two home runs in the same game, but he also beat every team in both the AL and the NL. He's got yet another dubious distinction in that he was traded not once, but twice, for future Hall of Famers.

WHAT A WAY FOR IT TO END

We've talked about exciting finishes, bizarre plays, and firsts. Now we must sadly have a "last," but I found a great one to end it on. One thing we didn't spend a lot of time on, and one that's often overlooked as to its impact on a game, is the stolen base.

Obviously taking a free base is a big deal, but if a known base-stealer is on base it really can intimidate the pitcher, who simply knows the runner is going to try and steal. It's just a question of when. Often times it seems players try to steal at inopportune times, or when it just doesn't seem to make sense.

Remember, they do get caught and give away an out, so even with tons of speed it's all about timing. Sometimes you just get the timing wrong.

So, in perhaps what was one of the most ill-advised attempts to steal a base, a World Series ended. If it had been anyone other than Babe Ruth himself, he'd still be being demonized for it.

Ruth reasoned that the pitcher, none other than the legendary Grover Alexander, was pitching too well and not paying enough attention to him at first base. Well, that may well have been true, but obviously the catcher was, so a World Series ended with a player getting gunned down at second base.

RANDOM FUN FACTS

1. We talked about how World War II had such an impact on baseball, but in at least one instance it was the other way around. The military designed the grenade to be the size and weight of a baseball, because "any young American man should be able to throw it."

2. The majority of the time in the All-Star game, or in the World Series, the Most Valuable Player is from the winning team. In the 1960 World Series Bobby Richardson hit .357 with 12 runs batted in. His team lost, but he won the MVP award.

3. Rock and Roll! Geddy Lee is the lead singer for the band Rush, a rock band from Canada that's still performing today. They were inducted into the Rock and Roll Hall of Fame in 2013. At one time Geddy had over 200 signed baseballs from the Negro Leagues, and in 2008 donated all of them to the Negro League Hall of Fame.

4. In 1989 Gayle Gardner became the first woman to regularly host Major League Baseball for a network. The National Broadcast Company.

5. Many have said that the most successful hitters have the ability to process visual information faster than others. That would make sense, since most good hitters are often heard

saying that they need to be able to pick up the spin of the ball to tell what kind of pitch it is.

6. Players had worn batting helmets for some time, but in 1983 they were required to wear one with a flap to protect the ear as well.

7. Ralph Kiner led the league in home runs for seven consecutive seasons, and they were the first seven years he played.

8. Hoyt Wilhelm had a 21-year career as a pitcher, and in his first at bat he hit a home run, the only one he would ever hit.

9. The year was 1978 and the game was between the Texas Rangers and the Baltimore Orioles. It's not here for what happen on the field, but off of it. George Medich was a Rangers' pitcher, who saved the life of a fan who was having a heart attack. George had studied medicine at the University of Pittsburgh, hence from then on he was known as "Doc" Medich.

10. Joe Sewell played most of his career with Cleveland, and ended it with a few years with the Yankees. In 1930 he had 353 at bats, striking out only three times. Two of them in the same game.

11. Long time baseball manager/broadcaster Bobby Valentine was tossed from a game in 1999. He changed into street clothes, donned a fake moustache, and came back to the dugout. He was fined $5000.

12. The first actual uniforms were worn by the Knickerbockers in 1839, complete with straw hats.

13. Jackie Mitchell was one of the first women pitchers. Pitching in a AA exhibition game against the New York Yankees, she struck out Babe Ruth and Lou Gehrig back-to-back. A few days later, Kenesaw Landis voided her contract and declared that baseball was too strenuous for women.

14. Pee Wee Reese was an All-Star shortstop for many years with the Dodgers, and played in 44 World Series games. All 44 were against the Yankees.

15. In 1990, the Twins finished 29 games out of first place, or in last place. The Braves finished 26 games out, or in last place. The following year they played each other in the World Series.

16. Between 1994-1996 the Chicago Cubs did not start a left-handed pitcher.

17. Ken Griffey, Jr and Stan Musial were both born in Donora, PA. Small world, but they were also both born on November 21st.

18. The Yankees were the first team to wear numbers on their backs. They did it based on their position in the batting order. Babe Ruth always batted third, hence, #3.

19. There are a lot of attendance records talked about, but rarely the smallest. It was actually in 2011 when the Marlins and Reds met in Miami. Hurricane Irene was off the coast, so the official attendance was 347.

20. Lastly, the oldest. Julio Franco hit a home run in April of 2006. He became the oldest player (47 years, 240 days) to ever hit one.

TEST YOURSELF – QUESTIONS AND ANSWERS

1. Who is the only pitcher to throw a perfect game and lose?

   A. Babe Ruth

   B. Sandy Koufax

   C. Harvey Haddix

2. Where was the first Major League game played outside of the US and Canada?

   A. Mexico

   B. Japan

   C. Australia

3. Where was the first Major League game played west of St. Louis?

   A. Los Angeles

   B. Seattle

   C. Kansas City

4. Who hit the first indoor home run?

   A. Ted Williams

   B. Mickey Mantle

   C. Craig Biggio

5. What famous ballpark is flanked by water, named McCovey Cove?

   A. AT & T Park
   B. Wrigley Field
   C. Ebbets Field

ANSWERS

1. C
2. A
3. C
4. B
5. A

DON'T FORGET YOUR FREE BOOKS

MORE BOOKS BY BILL O'NEILL

I hope you enjoyed this book and learned something new. Please feel free to check out some of my previous books on Amazon.